# ROOTS IN THE SKY

## A HISTORY OF BRITISH AEROSPACE AIRCRAFT

ROBERT MEDDEMMEN **DESIGNER**
PETER GARNIER FRSA **MANAGING EDITOR**
BRYAN CAMBRAY **PUBLISHER**

Published for *Flight International*
by IPC Transport Press, Special Publications Dept.
Dorset House Stamford Street London SE1 9LU,
with grateful acknowledgements to British Aerospace
and the Imperial War Museum for all their help
in providing information and photographs


**ISBN 0 617 00323 8**

**T**he history of British aviation seemingly turned full cycle in the Spring of 1977 when British Aerospace established its Corporate headquarters at Brooklands, Weybridge, Surrey. The new enterprise formed out of the Hawker Siddeley Aviation, and Dynamics companies, British Aircraft Corporation and Scottish Aviation and representing most of the firms which pioneered aeronautical development in this country, had returned to the place where it all began in the Summer of 1908.

For here at Brooklands, Alliott Verdon-Roe, a Manchester man became the first Englishman to fly a powered aircraft. The fence on which he tethered his flimsy machine remains. So does the famous AVRO name, later to become part of Hawker Siddeley Aviation. Marking the spot still stands a plaque erected by Vickers-Armstrongs, the inheritors of the site which became the centre for the British Aircraft Corporation.

And in a few sentences describing these two related events, we have swept through 70 years heritage now vested in our new company and embracing such famous names as Sopwith, Bristol, de Havilland, Glosters, English Electric, Blackburn and many more.

I am therefore pleased to introduce this new book which traces in detail that history both in words and pictures.

It is quite remarkable that so many developments have taken place in such a short time from "Stick and String" to Concorde and Harrier. It is also quite remarkable that so many of these developments have been British.

SIR FREDERICK W. PAGE
Chairman & Chief Executive
British Aerospace Aircraft Group
*Spring 1980*

# ROOTS IN THE SKY

**By OLIVER TAPPER**



**Opposite page:** *A Panavia Tornado GR1 prototype, in high-speed, low-level flight, with wings in the fully swept-back position. (Crown copyright)*

OLIVER TAPPER

*Sadly, we record that since his putting the last full-stop to this book, Oliver Tapper has died. Oliver had been ill for a year or so, nursed by his loving wife Hilary. He devoted himself to this work, which I think he sensed would be his last.*

*I knew him well, having been his junior editorial assistant in the 1950s on that stylish aviation publication* The de Havilland Gazette.

*Two sins he would not tolerate: pretentiousness and inaccuracy. He also detested verbal flabbiness; I daren't remember how many of my poor words he chopped ruthlessly out.*

*Oliver had a dry anecdote for every occasion, mostly drawn from his extensive flying experience. He was totally unflappable, whatever the provocation.*

*He learnt to fly at Stag Lane, and knew personally many of the great pioneers. As a result of his flying training his heart was always with "DH" and its great aeroplanes and people. He joined the de Havilland Aircraft Company in 1949, after a spell with Esso's aviation department.*

*In the 1930s he helped to set up the "AA" aviation department, and in British light aviation's golden years he was a familiar figure at all the events and races.*

*During the war he was a Lieutenant-Commander communications pilot in the Fleet Air Arm. His favourite picture, always reminding him of those days, is a lovely Wootton of a de Havilland Dragon Rapide flying over Scotland.*

*Like his wife Hilary, a competent pilot herself, and with whom I was a student in the de Havilland Aeronautical Technical School, Oliver Tapper was a total aviation person and an articulate writer, as this book testifies.*

*J. M. RAMSDEN*

# CONTENTS

*Artistic preview of the latest in the line—the new generation BAe 146 feederjet which will be in service in 1982. This aircraft is designed for economic operation from small airfields, will be powered by four Avco Lycoming ALF 502 engines, and will carry up to 104 passengers.*

# BRITISH AEROSPACE HERITAGE

When British Aerospace came into being in April 1977 with the merging of British Aircraft Corporation, Hawker Siddeley Aviation, Hawker Siddeley Dynamics and Scottish Aviation, it was a fitting climax to a long and distinguished record of pioneering achievements by British aircraft builders whose roots reach back to the early years of the century. It was then, and in the years that followed, that individuals and firms, whose names form the very essence of flying history, kept Britain in the forefront of aviation progress and who, in spite of daunting problems, laid a sure foundation on which British Aerospace is now established.

Credit for making the first move in this 70-year evolution must surely go to Alliott Verdon-Roe, a Manchester man who, at the age of 31, was the first Englishman to fly a powered aircraft. This historic flight, variously reported as being between 75 and 150 feet in length, took place on June 8, 1908 on the Brooklands motor racing track at Weybridge. This first hop, one of several made that day, was not considered worthy of recognition so Alliott Verdon-Roe, later Sir Alliott, was never officially credited with being the first Englishman to fly. However, no one can dispute his later claim to be the first man to fly over British soil in a British aeroplane powered by a British engine. This he accomplished on July 13, 1909, on Lea Marshes near London, in his "Avroplane", a small triplane with a 9hp J.A.P. engine. Happily,

*Built in a stable in the London suburb of Putney, A. V. Roe's first aeroplane was taken to Brooklands for trials. After taxying with a 9 hp JAP engine he borrowed a 24 hp Antoinette engine which enabled him to make several short hops to a height of 2 or 3 feet on June 8, 1908.*

*Sopwith Snipes in the erecting shop at the Ham factory in December 1918. With the signing of the armistice in November, most of these aircraft were destined never to fly. Subsequently, this same shop would house a succession of production runs ranging from Sea Furies to Harriers and Hawks.*

this famous aircraft is preserved for all time in London's Science Museum.

Later, in February 1910, Verdon-Roe sought financial help from his brother Humphrey and together they formed a private company with the intention of using some of the spare space in Humphrey's factory at Brownfield Mill, in Manchester for building aeroplanes. Three years later, in January 1913, A. V. Roe and Co., Ltd. was officially registered as a public company. Success became assured when, in 1913, the famous Avro 504 biplane emerged; this became the basic trainer for the R.F.C. and the R.A.F. from 1914 until 1932 and which gave first-flight "joy-rides" to many thousands between the wars.

### More to come

Hard on the heels of Verdon-Roe were other would-be airmen seeking to follow the lead given earlier by the Wright brothers in America. Two men who were neck-and-neck for second place were Robert Blackburn and Geoffrey de Havilland (later Sir Geoffrey), both of whom were busy during 1908 and 1909 building their own versions of flying machines. Blackburn appears to have achieved his first, underpowered hop on a sandy beach in Yorkshire in the spring of 1909. His machine was, however, badly damaged in the spring of 1910 when he attempted to make a turn. Geoffrey de Havilland first became airborne in December 1909 but his biplane broke up as soon as it left the ground and

*The Vickers Vimy bomber flown by John Alcock and Arthur Whitten Brown, seen leaving St. John's, Newfoundland, on June 14, 1919, at the start of the first ever non-stop trans-Atlantic flight. Early next morning the Vimy landed in an Irish bog. The time was 15 hours 57 minutes and the distance 1,890 miles.*

crashed immediately, the only salvable item being the engine which itself had been designed and built by de Havilland.

Both Blackburn and de Havilland, inspired by successful French designs, set about building fresh aircraft, Blackburn basing his new layout on the Antoinette monoplane, while de Havilland favoured the biplane configuration exploited by Farman. Both these new aircraft were successful; de Havilland first flew his biplane from a meadow near Newbury in September 1910, while Blackburn's monoplane was flown by B. C. Hucks from a beach near Filey on March 8, 1911.

Another pioneer of the period, T. O. M. Sopwith, later Sir Thomas, actually became airborne much earlier, in 1908, but that was in a balloon. He made several such flights, after one of which he landed in London's Regents Park but, because he was under 21 years of age he was refused a balloon pilot's certificate. Sopwith, who was also a keen motorist and yachtsman, soon turned his attention to aeroplanes and, in 1910, he bought a Howard Wright monoplane and taught himself to fly, gaining his Royal Aero Club aviator's certificate—No. 31, on November 21—within a month of his first

flight. Before this, on November 10, 1910, he broke two British records by flying a distance of 107¾ miles in 3 hours 12 minutes.

During 1911 Sopwith continued to add to his reputation as a pilot, especially by winning a number of flying competitions in America, and early in 1912 he opened a flying school at Brooklands which was responsible for training a number of budding airmen, including a certain Major Trenchard who six years later, as Major General Trenchard, founded the Royal Air Force. Later in 1912 Sopwith decided to concentrate on building aircraft, a step which, to say the least, was to have a significant influence on future events. For this purpose he set up a factory in a disused roller skating rink in Kingston-upon-Thames, and the Sopwith Aviation Co. Ltd. was officially registered in 1913. A young Australian, Harry Hawker, joined Sopwith as a mechanic on June 29, 1912. Later that year Sopwith taught him to fly. In Sopwith's own words "The pupil become the master of the art", and Hawker was promoted to what would today be called the Company's chief test pilot.

Meanwhile, Robert Blackburn had completed his third aircraft, the Mercury monoplane. This was exhibited at the 1911 Olympia Aero Show as the product of The Blackburn Aeroplane Company. During 1911

rather different pattern. Soon after the successful flights of his second aeroplane, he found himself running short of money and was therefore glad to accept, in December 1910, an appointment as designer and test pilot at the Royal Aircraft Factory (now the Royal Aircraft Establishment) at Farnborough. His biplane was bought by the Factory for £400 and it subsequently became the FE1, the first of a long line of Factory designs. In May 1914 de Havilland was persuaded to become chief designer of The Aircraft Manufacturing Co. Ltd., known for short as "Airco", which had been established by G. Holt Thomas near Hendon Aerodrome. Thereafter, the name de Havilland, and the intials DH, were to be associated with a series

British and Colonial Aeroplane Co. Ltd. was registered on February 19, 1910, with a capital of £25,000. At the same time, Sir George registered three other companies, each with a nominal capital of £100. It was one of these, The Bristol Aeroplane Co. Ltd., which took over the assets of the original company in 1920; apart from simplifying the company's name, this also had the effect of bringing about a useful reduction in the punishing post-war Excess Profit Tax which had already put several aircraft builders out of business.

In 1910 The British and Colonial Aeroplane Co. started operations in two large sheds hired from the tramway company situated some four miles north of Bristol at Filton.

Blackburn, like Sopwith, started a flying school and, in the same year, he established a factory in some disused stables in Leeds. During the spring of 1914, the factory was moved to the Olympia roller-skating rink in Roundhay Road with an adjacent aerodrome in Roundhay Park. In June 1914 The Blackburn Aeroplane and Motor Co. Ltd. was registered with the Olympia works as its head office, an address which was to last until 1929, when the company's activities were moved to the factory and aerodrome at Brough on the banks of the River Humber.

Geoffrey de Havilland's career followed a

of designs ranging from DH1 to DH125.

The Bristol company came into being in a way that was in marked contrast to that of most of its contemporaries; its origins stemmed, not from the labours of pioneer airmen struggling to get airborne, but from the considered actions of an established business man, Sir George White, who had already pioneered the electric tramway in his native city of Bristol. A display by French aviators witnessed by Sir George in France served to convince him that aviation had a future and he forthwith decided to form his own aircraft company. Thus it was that The

The original intention of building the French Zodiac biplane under licence was abandoned when the first specimen sent from France failed to fly. Subsequently, the company began building the famous Bristol Boxkite, based on the Farman biplane, which flew well and was sold in considerable numbers at home and overseas. By the time war broke out in 1914 an additional factory had been acquired at Brislington, a suburb of Bristol, and the company's capital had been increased to £250,000. The Boxkite proved to be an ideal primary trainer for the two flying schools established by the company at Larkhill, on

Salisbury Plain, and at Brooklands. These schools, between them, had trained more than 300 pupils by August 1914, representing nearly half the total number of British pilot's certificates issued by the Royal Aero Club up to that time.

Of the two great rivals in the armament business, Sir W. G. Armstrong Whitworth and Co. and Vickers Sons and Maxim, it was the latter that first entered the aviation field, having been asked in 1908 by the Admiralty to build a rigid airship on the lines of the German Zeppelin. Construction began in 1909, but a total lack of experience in airship construction resulted in long delays and the airship, unofficially known as the Mayfly was not completed until 1911; it was this same lack of experience which led to the vessel breaking her back in September 1911 without ever having flown.

In spite of the Mayfly failure, Vickers went ahead with the formation of an aviation department in 1911 and, like Bristols, at first pinned their faith in a French design, acquiring a licence to build the REP monoplane. The first of these was purchased in France, modified by Vickers, and tested at Joyce Green Aerodrome near Dartford in Kent on the banks of the River Thames. Also in 1911, the company, which had recently adopted the shortened title of Vickers Ltd., opened a flying school at Brooklands where, in 1915, they moved their aircraft factory from its original location at Erith in Kent.

### Pusher biplanes

After building several variants of the first monoplane and a few experimental biplanes on Farman lines, Vickers produced a series of pusher aircraft, including the FB4, a gun-carrying biplane which was exhibited at the 1913 Olympia Aero Show in London. This was followed by the FB5, which became known as the Gunbus, Britain's first practical fighting aeroplane. This gave a good account of itself during the early months of the war in 1914 until it was eventually eclipsed by the arrival of the German Fokker monoplane. At the war's end Vickers produced the twin-engined Vimy, considered to be the best bomber of its day, which later achieved the first non-stop flight across the Atlantic and the first flight from England to Australia.

In 1913 the firm of Sir W. G. Armstrong Whitworth and Co. Ltd. decided to form an "aerial department" having been approached by both the Admiralty and the War Office, the former inviting tenders for rigid and non-rigid airships and the latter asking the company to build aeroplanes. One of the aerial department's first actions was to purchase land at Barlow, in Yorkshire, for the erection of an airship factory. The first aeroplane plant was located in one of the company's buildings at Scotswood in Newcastle-upon-Tyne, and it was here that the first small, Farnborough designed batch of BE2s were built in 1913 for the War Office. Later in 1913 Armstrong Whitworth acquired a disused roller-skating rink at

Gosforth, to the north of Newcastle, as a factory. With the outbreak of war and the receipt of further orders for BE2c aircraft the Gosforth factory was enlarged and an aerodrome was established on a nearby corner of Newcastle's Town Moor. Armstrong Whitworth's main contribution to the 1914-18 war was the FK8, a sturdy, dependable biplane which was used extensively for artillery observation and photography on the Western Front.

Elsewhere in this country other personalities and firms were heading, all unsuspecting, towards the mainstream of aviation activity and, eventually, to British Aerospace. In Coventry, a young racing cyclist named John Siddeley, who was the first man to cycle from Land's End to John O' Groats, graduated to motor engineering and, in 1902, formed the Siddeley Autocar Co. to market a four-cylinder car of his own design. Its success led eventually to the formation of the Siddeley Deasy Motor Car Co. with works at Parkside in Coventry. The company did not become involved in aviation until after the outbreak of war in 1914, but John Siddeley subsequently played an important part in the development of British aviation and was raised to the peerage, becoming Lord Kenilworth in 1937.

Another personality whose name is now largely forgotten, but who certainly started something, was Noel Pemberton-Billing. Well known before the war as a wealthy motorist and yachtsman, he was both enterprising and unorthodox. In 1913, for a bet of £500, he learned to fly and qualified for his aviator's certificate, not only in one day, but actually before breakfast; nobody would hire him an aeroplane for this escapade, so he bought a Farman biplane specially for the purpose. His instructor was Barnwell of the Vickers flying school at Brooklands.

The firm of Pemberton-Billing Ltd. was

*Above: On August 25, 1919, a DH16 of Aircraft Transport & Travel left Hounslow Aerodrome with four passengers at 12.30 pm for Paris. Ten minutes later, a DH4a with two passengers, took off from Le Bourget for London. Both flights arrived without incident, thus inaugurating the world's first regular international air service.*

registered in the summer of 1914, its founder having already set up a factory at Woolston on Southampton Water, in which he planned to build "boats that could fly rather than aeroplanes that could float". In line with these ideas he chose, as the factory's telegraphic address the name "Supermarine". The firm's first flying boat, the PB 1, a tractor biplane, was shown at the 1914 Olympia Aero Show. It is believed that this boat never flew but, by a stretch of the imagination, it can be seen as a distant forebear of the Walrus amphibian that became so famous in World War 2. Later, Pemberton-Billing joined the Royal Naval Air Service and, in 1916, he sold his interest in his company which then changed its name to The Supermarine Aviation Works Ltd.

### Demands of war

The outbreak of war in 1914 changed everything for the aircraft industry, if such it could be called at that time; almost overnight it graduated from an apprenticeship to big business and aeroplane production rocketed. In the first ten months of the war, to May 1915, 530 aircraft were built in British factories, whereas during the last ten months of hostilities the figure had risen to 26,685. In fact, the great majority of these aircraft were built by firms who, previous to 1914, had no connection with aviation; for instance, of some 18,000 Sopwith aeroplanes of various types built during the war, all but 3,300 were built by sub-contractors.

One of the sub-contracting companies which showed an interest in continuing with aircraft construction in the future was H. H. Martyn and Co. Ltd. of Cheltenham, a firm with an established reputation for high-class woodwork. The company had been recruited by Holt Thomas of Airco to undertake sub-contract work. In this it was highly successful, so much so, that Holt Thomas and A. W. Martyn, decided jointly to form a separate aviation company. Thus it was that in June 1917 it was registered The Gloucestershire Aircraft Co. Ltd.

By 1918 the Gloucestershire company was fully engaged in building Bristol Fighters and Nieuport Nighthawk single-seat fighters, the latter being a product of The Nieuport and General Aircraft Co. This firm, like so many others after the war, was forced to close in 1920 and Gloucestershire Aircraft, with considerable foresight, acquired not only a quantity of Nighthawk components, which later were to form the basis for a large export order of fighters to Japan, but also, and more important, it recruited Nieuport's chief designer, H. P. Folland, another name which contributed significantly to the build-up towards British Aerospace. Henry Folland, like de Havilland, had been a designer at Farnborough where he was largely responsible for the SE5, which vied with the Sopwith Camel as the R.F.C.'s most successful war-time fighter. With Gloucestershire Aircraft, Folland was responsible for a series of elegant record-breaking aeroplanes and seaplanes which only just failed to achieve victory in the Schneider Trophy contests.

In the euphoria which followed the armistice in November 1918, there was much optimism about the future of aviation, but the abrupt cancellation of all military orders meant a rapid end to many cherished ambitions. Even some of the most successful manufacturers failed to survive the twin blows of cancelled orders and the excess profit taxes which were levied on them. In 1920 Holt Thomas was forced to sell the Airco company to the Birmingham Small Arms organisation which soon decided to close down the aviation section. About the same time the Sopwith company, while still solvent, went into voluntary liquidation, and the company was wound up in September 1920.

But neither de Havilland nor Sopwith were the sort of men to let matters rest there: de Havilland, with generous help from Holt Thomas and with some of his own money, was able to scrape together enough capital to form his own company which was registered as The de Havilland Aircraft Co. Ltd. on September 25, 1920. As the new company became established at the works and aero-

drome at Stag Lane, not far from Hendon, de Havilland soon found himself becoming impatient with the official Air Ministry contract and specification procedures for military aircraft, and he chose to follow his natural instinct and to concentrate mainly on civil aircraft, notably, the Moth series of light aircraft which finally served to put the company in a sound financial position.

Thomas Sopwith registered his new company on November 15, 1920 and called it H. G. Hawker Engineering Co. Ltd. after the

*Left: On June 30, 1926, Alan Cobham set out to survey the route to Australia in a DH50J seaplane. After an adventurous journey over sections of the route where no facilities of any sort existed, he reached Melbourne on August 15 and arrived back in London on October 1 alighting on the Thames.*

*Below: Four Southampton II flying boats of the RAF Far East Flight at moorings in Sydney Harbour, Australia. The cruise started from England in October 1927 and, after circling Australia, arrived back at Singapore in September 1928. During the cruise the boats covered some 28,000 miles and alighted at 63 different places.*

*Right: Three Wellesleys of the RAF Long Range Development Flight took off from Ismailia in Egypt on on November 5, 1938. Heading towards Australia, the three aircraft beat the existing record when passing the island of Celebes. Subsequently, one aircraft landed at Kupang, but two reached Darwin establishing a new record of 7,157.7 miles.*

*A Harrier VTOL jet landing at a disused coal yard outside London's St. Pancras Station after flying in the Transatlantic Air Race on May 9, 1969. The pilot checked into the race control centre 5 hours 50 minutes after taking off from the vicinity of New York's Empire State Building.*

Sopwith test pilot whose name was almost as well known as Sopwith's. Hawker was famous both for his exploits before the war and for his almost miraculous rescue in mid-Atlantic after his failure, in May 1919, to achieve the first non-stop crossing of the Atlantic. Harry Hawker did not live long to serve the company bearing his name; he was killed near Hendon on July 12, 1921, when his Nieuport Goshawk crashed while practising for the Aerial Derby. In 1924 a young draughtsman named Sydney Camm joined Hawkers and, in 1925 when the post fell vacant, he was made chief designer. He soon demonstrated his exceptional ability with a series of outstanding military aeroplanes: he was knighted in 1953. In 1933 Hawker formed itself into a public company and took the opportunity of simplifying its name to Hawker Aircraft Ltd.

Armstrong Whitworth's transition to peace followed a more complicated pattern. After the abrupt cancellation of orders this Newcastle firm, which had built more than 1,200 aeroplanes and three rigid airships, announced the closure of its aviation department in October 1919. But, in the meantime, at John Siddeley's instigation, Armstrong Whitworth had bought up the Siddeley Deasy company, which had itself been manufacturing aircraft as well as aero engines, in Coventry. Most of the aircraft built were of Government design, but in 1918 a new prototype fighter was built called the Siddeley Siskin. Following the purchase a new subsidiary company was formed called Armstrong Whitworth Development Co. Ltd. This had two subsidiaries called Armstrong Siddeley Motors Ltd. and Sir W. G. Armstrong Whitworth Aircraft Co. Ltd., all with headquarters in Coventry.

Under Siddeley's direction the Coventry enterprises prospered in spite of the hard times; in contrast, the parent company in Newcastle continued to languish. Not satisfied with this position, Siddeley made a bold decision and offered to buy the Armstrong

Development Co., and its subsidiaries for £1,500,000, and the sale was concluded in December 1926. In March 1927 the name of the holding company was changed to the Armstrong Siddeley Development Co. Ltd. with its two subsidiaries retaining their names. In Newcastle the fortunes of the original Armstrong Whitworth company continued to decline until, in 1927, the rivalry between the two armament giants was finally resolved when Vickers took over Armstrong Whitworth under the title of Vickers-Armstrong Ltd.

## Shedding the load

Before the war, in 1912, the Coventry Ordnance Works had made some experimental aeroplanes of their own design; these played but a small part in pre-war aviation, but during the war the firm had built quantities of other people's aeroplanes. In 1918 Coventry Ordnance and The Phoenix Dynamo Manufacturing Co. of Bradford, which built flying boats for the government, amalgamated and, with three other companies, Dick Kerr and Co. of Preston, Willans and Robinson Ltd., of Rugby and the Siemens Dynamo Works, of Stafford, joined forces to form The English Electric Co. Ltd. After the armistice in 1918 the new company continued to produce successful prototypes, mostly flying boats but, with no prospect of production orders, decided, in 1926, to close its aircraft department temporarily. The first designer of note associated with English Electric's aircraft activities was W. O. Manning.

The closure lasted longer than expected, and it was not until 1938 that the department was re-activated with large contracts to build Handley Page bombers. After the war English Electric established its own design organisation led by W. E. W. "Teddy" Petter which produced two highly successful military aircraft, the Canberra bomber and the Lightning supersonic fighter of 1954, which, over 25 years later was still in front-line operational service with the R.A.F. In January 1959 a wholly-owned subsidiary named English Electric Aviation Ltd. was formed to take over the parent company's aircraft and guided weapon activities.

In the years between the wars the other major manufacturers which formed the background for British Aerospace, namely Avro,

Blackburn, Bristol, de Havilland, Folland, Hawker, Supermarine, and Vickers continued for a time to survive and retain their own individuality. But not for long: in 1920 the Avro company, while retaining its name and identity, became a wholly-owned subsidiary of the Crossley Motor Group.

In 1927 Crossley sold the Avro Company to John Siddeley. In the same year Sir Alliott Verdon-Roe severed his connection with Avro to take a controlling interest in the long-established firm of S. E. Saunders Ltd. which built boats and flying boats in the Isle of Wight. Subsequently, in 1926, the firm, by then known as Saunders-Roe Ltd., became a partly-owned subsidiary of de Havilland but, in the reorganisation of 1959, it was sold to the Westland Aircraft Co.

### The embryo Spitfire

At Southampton, Supermarines were doing well; in 1920 Reginald Mitchell, who had joined the company in 1917, was made chief designer and his outstanding successes in the Schneider Trophy contests were of great benefit to the company and, indeed, to the nation. Mitchell, whose Spitfire fighter will always be his memorial, did not live long enough to receive the honours he so richly deserved. In 1928 Vickers, which had that year turned its aviation department into a subsidiary company called Vickers (Aviation) Ltd., wished to expand its aviation business and thus acquired the Supermarine company. The team at Southampton remained the same and it was not until 1931 that the name was changed to The Supermarine Aviation Works (Vickers) Ltd. In 1938 this subsidiary, as well as Vickers (Aviation) Ltd., were absorbed into Vickers-Armstrong Ltd.

Meanwhile, the Gloucestershire Aircraft Company's salesmen, who had been achieving a considerable export business with Folland-designed fighters, had become tired of trying to explain to overseas customers the correct pronunciation of "Gloucestershire". It was therefore decided, in 1926, to change the company's name to Gloster Aircraft Ltd. For a time the company continued to prosper with its Grebe and Gamecock fighters, but from 1932 onwards business declined and, when Hawkers, looking for more production capacity, made a take-over bid, Glosters were pleased to accept and the deal was completed in the spring of 1934. In 1937 Folland resigned and his place as chief designer was taken by George Carter, who came from Hawkers *via* de Havilland, and who was subsequently responsible for designing the Gloster E28/39, Britain's first jet aircraft, which flew for the first time in May 1941.

The next big deal occurred in July 1935 when Sir John Siddeley, as he had then become, suddenly decided to sell his companies to Hawkers, with the result that a new company was formed called Hawker Siddeley Aircraft Co. Ltd.; and so, for the first time, the two great names came together in what was soon to become known as the Hawker Siddeley Group, which by then included Hawker Aircraft, Armstrong Whitworth

Aircraft, Armstrong Siddeley Motors as well as Avros and Glosters.

The 1930s saw the formation of a number of companies which, although their names are now largely forgotten, played their part in the heritage of British Aerospace. First came Airspeed Ltd., formed on the slenderest of resources in 1931. The company struggled to survive in a highly competitive environment until it was rescued by Swan Hunter, the shipbuilding firm which formed a new company called Airspeed (1934) Ltd. During the war Airspeed, as well as designing and building the Oxford twin-engined trainer and Horsa troop-carrying glider, did a considerable amount of sub-contract work for de Havilland, and it was this close association which led to Airspeed being purchased by de Havilland in 1940. In June 1951 the merger became complete and the firm became the Airspeed Division of de Havilland.

Another small company formed in 1931 was General Aircraft Ltd. which eventually became established at Hanworth Aerodrome in Middlesex. During the war the company designed and built the Hamilcar tank-carrying glider and, after the war, the G.A.L.60 Universal Freighter. This became the Blackburn Beverley transport when Blackburn merged with General Aircraft to become

Blackburn and General Aircraft Ltd. in January 1949. In 1932 Edgar Percival formed his own company to market the Vega Gull monoplane which was proving popular with private owners. The Percival Aircraft Co. eventually established a factory adjoining Luton Aerodrome from which, before long, emerged large numbers of the military version of the Vega Gull, the Percival Proctor. In 1944 the company became part of the Hunting Group and in 1954 the name was changed, firstly, to Hunting Percival Aircraft Ltd. and then, in 1957 to Hunting Aircraft Ltd.

**Two more names**
The year 1935 saw the formation of two other new companies which were to play their part in the genesis of British Aerospace. After being formed at Hamble, near Southampton, as British Marine Aircraft Ltd., the company underwent reorganisation in 1937 with H. P. Folland as managing director and, in the same year, the name was changed to Folland Aircraft Ltd. After being engaged throughout the war on sub-contract work, the company began work in 1951 on a private-venture light fighter, the Midge, from which was developed the Gnat trainer for the R.A.F.

Finally, in June 1935, the Marquess of Clydesdale (later the Duke of Hamilton) and

David McIntyre, who together in April 1933 had succeeded in flying over the summit of Mount Everest, were instrumental in forming Scottish Aviation Ltd. and establishing Prestwick Aerodrome, which later became the terminal of the wartime Atlantic ferry organisation. Starting with a flying school, which continued to operate until 1941, Scottish Aviation opened its first factory in 1938 for the purpose of undertaking overhaul and sub-contract work. By 1941, in much enlarged premises, the company was engaged in the modification of imported U.S. aircraft and repair work on other combat aircraft.

After the war Scottish Aviation produced two designs of their own, the Pioneer and the Twin Pioneer, both of which served with the R.A.F.; subsequently, the firm took over the development and production of the Jetstream light transport, following the collapse of

*On October 24, 1975, the first-ever landing in fog by a passenger-carrying airliner in scheduled service was made at London Airport Heathrow, by a British Airways Trident using a system which, after extensive testing, received official approval earlier in the year. Category III conditions (visibility 200 metres) prevailed and all other airliners were diverted.*

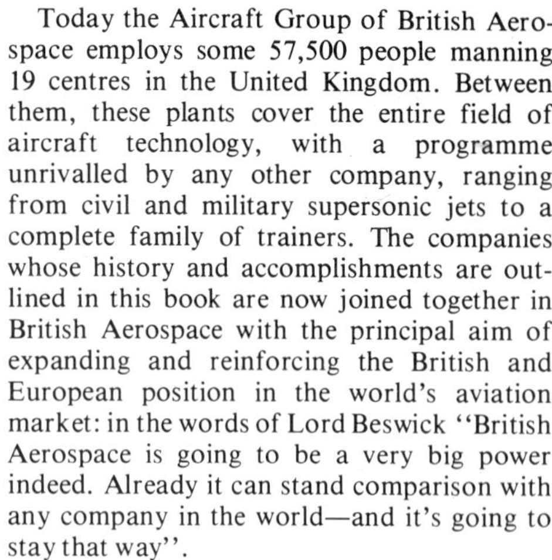

Handley Page, and the Bulldog trainer from Beagle. In 1966 Scottish Aviation became a member of the Cammell Laird Group.

In the years between the wars the larger manufacturers tended to specialise to some extent. Avro built many trainers while Vickers was noted for its night bombers; Armstrong Whitworth and Hawkers built mostly fighters, general-purpose aircraft and light bombers while Bristol and Glosters concentrated mainly on fighters. Supermarine specialised in flying boats—and racing seaplanes—with Blackburn adding its quota of marine aircraft but tending more towards carrier-borne aircraft for the Fleet Air Arm. Most of the firms made some attempts at producing civil aircraft but de Havilland were the most prominent in this field.

The war, when it came, tended to crystalise the situation and, in retrospect, it is fair to say that the name of each firm became mainly synonymous with a particular type. In the case of Avro it was the Lancaster bomber, while Vickers and Armstrong Whitworth will

*Concordes of British Airways and Air France meet at Washington Airport on January 21, 1976, after having jointly inaugurated the first supersonic air service across the Atlantic between Europe and the USA. Later, the New York authorities agreed to receive Concorde and services from London and Paris commenced on November 22, 1977.*

always be associated with, respectively, the Wellington and the Whitley. The names Hawker and Supermarine are inevitably linked as the makers of the Hurricanes and Spitfires which won the Battle of Britain, while de Havilland's outstanding contribution was the Mosquito. To Naval airmen Blackburn is synonymous with the Skua dive-bomber, while Bristol is famous for the Blenheim and the Beaufighter. Finally, the name Gloster recalls vividly the early exploits of the Gladiator and, later, the Meteor, Britain's first operational jet fighter.

The end of the second world war marked the beginning of the most significant technical revolution since the Wright brothers' exploits —the advent of the gas-turbine power plant, a field in which Great Britain held an undoubted lead. It coincided with a period of continuing international tension during which the world's air forces needed to re-equip, particularly with jet fighters which British factories were well placed to supply,

with large numbers of Meteors, Vampires and Hunters being delivered, not only to the R.A.F., but to numerous other air forces. Two British combat aircraft, the Canberra and, later, the Harrier shared the rare distinction of being adopted by United States forces. In the civil field, Britain led the way with the world's first turbo-propeller airliner, the Viscount, and the worlds first operational jet airliner, the Comet which, in a developed form, operated the first regular jet service between London and New York.

In spite of these successes it had long been apparent that a measure of rationalisation of the industry was inevitable; already the Hawker Siddeley Group (which by then incorporated Armstrong Whitworth, Avro, Gloster and Hawkers) represented a considerable consolidation. Thus it was, in accordance with government policy, the Group additionally acquired the Blackburn, Folland and de Havilland companies in January 1960. In 1963 the aerospace interests were divided into two companies, Hawker Siddeley Aviation and Hawker Siddeley Dynamics which subsequently came under the Group Chairmanship of Sir Arnold Hall. Again, in conformity with the wishes of the Government, the British Aircraft Corporation was formed in 1960, bringing together Bristol Aircraft, English Electric Aviation, Vickers Armstrong (Aircraft) Ltd., and Hunting Aircraft. In 1964 the Corporation was further consolidated by the

formation of British Aircraft Corporation (Operating) Ltd., under the chairmanship of Sir George Edwards who led the design teams for post-war Vickers aircraft.

The intention to merge these two large organisations had been mooted as early as 1967, but ten years were to elapse before this became an accomplished fact. A bill entitled "The Aircraft and Shipbuilding Industry Bill" was put before Parliament and, after a long debate, was passed, receiving the Royal Assent on March 17, 1977. Vesting day was named as April 29, 1977, on which the merged companies became the British Aerospace Corporation, with Lord Beswick, who had for some time been chairman of the organising committee, confirmed as chairman of the new state-owned enterprise.

British Aerospace emerges as the largest aircraft, missile and spacecraft company outside the United States and Russia, with a technical capacity unequalled by any other single company.

Today the Aircraft Group of British Aerospace employs some 57,500 people manning 19 centres in the United Kingdom. Between them, these plants cover the entire field of aircraft technology, with a programme unrivalled by any other company, ranging from civil and military supersonic jets to a complete family of trainers. The companies whose history and accomplishments are outlined in this book are now joined together in British Aerospace with the principal aim of expanding and reinforcing the British and European position in the world's aviation market: in the words of Lord Beswick "British Aerospace is going to be a very big power indeed. Already it can stand comparison with any company in the world—and it's going to stay that way".

*I*N the pages which follow will be found 250 photographs depicting a selection of the aircraft built by the founder companies of British Aerospace. Many of the types illustrated will be well known and some have stamped their names on history, but a large number, consisting of prototypes and experimental aircraft, will be less familiar. These latter types, mostly 'one-off', besides being of technical interest, are important because they formed an essential element of the research and development process which kept Great Britain in the forefront of aeronautical progress.

*The reasons why so many prototypes never reached the production line were many and various: some failed to come up to expectations; others, although first-class aircraft, were faced by even better competitors; still others were passed over because official requirements changed before they had a chance to show their paces. But, whatever the reason, they all made their contribution to aviation knowledge and orders for them often served to keep an impoverished industry alive between production orders.*

*The pictures are arranged in chronological order according to the best information available on first-flight dates, with the year of the aircraft's appearance heading the caption. Performance figures and other technical statistics mostly make dull reading and are omitted unless they are of particular significance, but the maximum weight and the wing span (or length, whichever is the greater) are included to give scale to the pictures.*

# IN THE BEGINNING

## 1909: Avroplane

The first all-British aeroplane to fly was this small triplane built by Alliott Verdon Roe. With a 9hp, twin-cylinder, air-cooled JAP engine the Avroplane, as it was first called, was tried out on the Lea Marshes in North East London and by July 1909 had achieved flights of 900 feet and more. Fore-and-aft control of the triplane was by altering the incidence of the mainplanes, the tail surfaces being fixed. Maximum weight (approx.) 450 lb; span 20 feet. *(below)*

## 1910: Roe III

Roe followed up his early success with the Roe III, pictured above. This was a big advance on its predecessors: the wings were fixed and control was by tail elevators, while ailerons replaced the earlier wing-warping arrangement. The engine was an eight-cylinder air-cooled V JAP developing 35hp. The Type III was Roe's first two-seater and one of the first passengers he carried was his mother. One Roe III was exported to America. Maximum weight (approx.) 750 lb; span 31 feet.

## 1909: Blackburn Monoplane

Built by Robert Blackburn in a small workshop in Leeds, this monoplane, with its builder at the controls, made brief hops along the sands at Marske in Yorkshire but it is doubtful if it ever really flew. It was smashed in May 1910 when Blackburn made a tentative effort to turn. The engine was a 35hp four-cylinder, water-cooled Green with chain drive to the propeller. Maximum weight (approx.) 800 lb; span 24 feet. *(above)*

### 1910: de Havilland's Second

Geoffrey de Havilland built his first aeroplane, and its engine, in 1909, but it was wrecked on the first attempt to fly. The second aeroplane, *shown below,* flew successfully in September 1910. De Havilland sold this machine to the Royal Aircraft Factory at Farnborough and was himself taken on as designer and test

than 20 being sold abroad. Others were used as trainers at the Bristol schools at Larkhill and Brooklands. Maximum weight 1,050 lb; span 34 feet 6 inches. *(bottom right)*

### 1911: Vickers' First

Vickers' first aeroplane was built under licence from the French firm Robert Esnault Pelterie

pilot. In 1914 he became chief designer for the Aircraft Manufacturing Company which produced the wartime de Havilland aeroplanes. Maximum weight (approx.) 1,000 lb; span 33 feet 6 inches.

### 1910: Bristol Boxkite

Unofficially called the Boxkite, this was the first successful aeroplane built by the British and Colonial Aeroplane Company. It was a copy of the French Farman biplane and was usually powered by a 50hp Gnome engine. The Boxkite remained in production until 1914, by which some 76 aircraft had been completed with more

(REP); the rear fuselage being made of steel tube, was of French construction with the rest of the aircraft built by Vickers. It crashed soon after its first flight but was followed by seven other Vickers-built monoplanes which, although strong, were not spectacular performers; they were, however, notable for being early examples of part-metal construction. Maximum weight (No. 7 of the series) 1,200 lb; span 34 feet 6 inches. *(top)*

### 1911: Avro Type D

The first of a long line of Avro biplanes, the Type D, was a two-seater with a Green engine of 35hp. A Type D biplane was

used for seaplane-float experiments at Barrow-in-Furness and, in 1912, this aircraft became the first seaplane ever to fly from British waters. The Avro flying school at Brooklands and later at Shoreham used aircraft of this type where they remained in service until 1914. Maximum weight (approx.) 500 lb; span 31 feet. *(centre left)*

### 1912: Avro Type 500

Thought by A. V. Roe to be his first really successful aeroplane, the Type 500 was the forerunner of the famous 504 series of trainers. A Type 500, with a 50hp Gnome rotary engine, underwent trials at Farnborough and performed so well that the War Office ordered two with dual controls. The Avro 500 soon established itself as the best available trainer and further orders followed from both the War Office and the Admiralty. Maximum weight (approx.) 1,300 lb; span 36 feet. *(right)*

### 1912: Sopwith Wright Biplane

The first of a long line of Sopwith-built aeroplanes was this Sopwith Wright flown by T. O. M. Sopwith at Brooklands. Reconstructed from a Burgess Wright biplane, the Sopwith Wright had a 35hp four-cylinder Green engine and, piloted by Harry Hawker in October 1912, it won the British Empire Michelin Trophy and a prize of £500 by remaining airborne for eight hours 23 minutes. At the same time it also established a new British endurance record. Span 38 feet 9 inches. *"Flight" photo. (above left)*

### 1912: Avro Type F

Probably the first aeroplane in the world in which the pilot was totally enclosed; He had a rather restricted view forwards and sideways through celluloid panels. The Avro Type F performed well but its 35hp Viale five-cylinder radial engine was not reliable, and after being damaged twice in forced landings, the one and only Type F monoplane was abandoned. Maximum weight (approx.) 800 lb; span 28 feet. *"Flight" photo. (above top)*

### 1912: Blackburn Single-Seat Monoplane

One of the most successful of several early aeroplanes built by Blackburns was the single-seat monoplane illustrated above. With a 50hp Gnome rotary engine it made a number of creditable flights until it was damaged in a bad landing in 1914. In 1938 it was discovered in a barn in Lincolnshire and was then restored to flying condition by the Shuttleworth Trust with which it resides today as the oldest flyable British aircraft. Maximum weight 980 lb; span 32 feet 1 inch. *(above)*

### 1913: Sopwith Tractor Biplane

A Sopwith exhibit at the 1913 Aero Show was this tractor biplane, fitted with a 80hp Gnome engine, in which Harry Hawker subsequently broke several records. In June 1913 he reached 12,900 feet with one passenger and later, in July, he flew the same machine, this time with three passengers, to the world-record height of 8,400 feet. The Sopwith tractor was used by both the R.F.C. and the R.N.A.S. who took it to France in August 1914. Maximum weight 1,550 lb; span 40 feet. *(Opposite page top left)*

### 1913: Avro 504K

This aircraft, and its many variants, remained in service with the R.F.C. and the R.A.F. from 1913 until the 504N was declared obsolete 20 years later. Most prolific of the series were the 504J, and the 504K illustrated above. The latter was used in great numbers during the First World War and, in civilian guise, right up to 1935 for giving joyrides all over Great Britain. Maximum weight (Avro 504K) 1,800 lb; span 36 feet. *(right)*

### 1913: Sopwith Bat Boat

Britain's first practical flying boat; first appeared at the 1913 Olympia Aero Show. Later in the year, with a Green engine of 100hp and flown by Harry Hawker, it won a prize of £500 for being the first British aircraft to make twelve alightings alternatively on land and water within the space of five hours. It was subsequently purchased by the Admiralty and took part in the Royal Naval Review of 1914. Maximum weight 1,700 lb; span 41 feet. *"Flight"* photo. *(left)*

### 1913: Sopwith Tabloid

The third Sopwith aeroplane to appear in 1913 was a small biplane known as the Tabloid. Powered by an 80hp Gnome engine, it made a dramatic appearance at Hendon in November 1913 where its speed and manoeuvrability amazed the onlookers. The Tabloid's most spectacular achievement was, as a seaplane seen above, winning the Schneider Trophy contest in 1914, but its real significance was that it pointed the way to the single-seater fighter. Maximum weight (landplane) 1,060 lb; span 25 feet 6 inches. *(above)*

# 1914: THE GREAT WAR

**1914: Vickers FB5 Gunbus**

During 1913 Vickers built a series of gun-carrying pusher biplanes culminating in the FB5, the Gunbus, which, armed with a single Lewis gun, became the first fighting aeroplane of the 1914-18 war. The FB5 first went into action on Christmas Day, 1914, against a German seaplane which flew up the Thames towards London. Later, on the Western Front, the Gunbus gave the R.F.C. a measure of air supremacy until the Fokker monoplane arrived in 1915. Maximum weight 2,050 lb; span 36 feet 6 inches. *(above)*

**1914: Sopwith Admiralty Seaplane Type 860**

Powered by a 225hp Sunbeam water-cooled engine, it was designed to carry a 14-inch torpedo weighing some 800 lb, and was built in two versions, one of which had a lower wing of shorter span; the wings were designed to fold. The Sopwith 860 was built in small numbers, but the type remained in service at least until 1916. *(top)*

**1915: De Havilland DH2**

The first two de Havilland designs to be built by the Aircraft Manufacturing Company at Hendon, the DH1 and the DH2, were pushers. The DH1 was a two-seater used mostly for training, but the DH2, pictured above, was a fighter that proved an effective answer to the hitherto dominant Fokker monoplane. The DH2 also served in the Middle East and at home against the Zeppelins. The engine was a 100hp Gnome. Maximum weight 1,440 lb; span 28 feet 3 inches *(right)*

### 1915: Armstrong Whitworth FK3

The Armstrong Whitworth firm started making government-designed BE aircraft in 1914, but the firm's designer, Frederick Koolhoven, believed he could improve on the official design. The resulting Armstrong Whitworth FK3 which, with a 105hp RAF engine, the same as that of the BE2c, had a better performance and was easier to build. Large numbers of FK3s were built but they did not supplant the official favourite. Maximum weight 2,050 lb; span 40 feet 1 inch. *Imperial War Museum photo. (top).*

### 1915: Bristol Scout

Types C and D were similar and, like the Sopwith Tabloid, can be considered as forerunners of the single-seat fighter. Fitted with a Gnome or Le Rhone engine of some 80hp, the Scout D had a top speed of more than 100 mph. A total of 371 Scouts was built during the war for both the R.F.C. and the R.N.A.S. They were used in France, Palestine, Mesopotamia and at home for anti-Zeppelin patrols. Maximum weight 2,050 lb; span 24 feet 7 inches. *(above centre)*

### 1916: Twin Blackburn

Known as the Blackburn TB, this aircraft was built to Admiralty order for anti-Zeppelin use, to be armed with steel incendiary darts. Of unconventional layout, with two fuselages as well as two engines, it was the first Blackburn type to be ordered into production, nine having been built. Fitted with either Gnome or Clerget engines. The TB seaplanes were underpowered and were never used for their designed purpose. Maximum weight 3,500 lb; span 60 feet 6 inches. *(above)*

### 1915: Sopwith Baby

The Royal Navy's need for a seaplane scout led to the production of the Sopwith Baby, an improved version of the Schneider Trophy winner. With a Clerget engine of either 110hp or 130hp, the Baby was built in large numbers by the Sopwith and Blackburn companies. It served throughout the war in the important, but unspectacular tasks of patrolling and escorting in the North Sea armed, mostly, with a Lewis gun and two 65 lb bombs. Maximum weight 1,700 lb; span 25 feet 8 inches. *(above)*

### 1915: Sopwith "1½-Strutter"

Probably so named because of the unusual arrangement of the centre-section struts, served on the Western Front and performed a variety of duties including bombing, fighting, photography and reconnaissance. The 1½-Strutter, a two-seater with a Clerget engine, was the first British aircraft to have a gun firing through the propeller. Large numbers were supplied to the French, Belgians, Russians and Italians. Maximum weight 2,150 lb; span 33 feet 6 inches. *(centre above)*

### 1916: Sopwith Pup

The first Sopwith single-seat fighter was quickly nicknamed the Pup and, in spite of strong official disapproval, the name stuck. The Pup, a delightful aeroplane to fly, was fitted with a variety of 80 to 100hp rotary engines but in spite of its low power it was more than a match for contemporary enemy fighters and its ability to maintain its height in combat enabled it to hold its own until the end of 1917. Maximum weight 1,225 lb; span 26 feet 6 inches. *Imperial War Museum photo. (below)*

### 1916: Sopwith Triplane

Designed to provide a high degree of manoeuvrability and to give the pilot a good view, the Sopwith Triplane, with a 130hp Clerget engine was an excellent performer and could out-climb the opposing enemy fighters. Used mainly by the R.N.A.S., the Triplane acquired a formidable reputation for invincibility that was, perhaps, not altogether justified. Nevertheless, two famous Triplane squadrons, "Naval Eight" and "Naval Ten" created havoc among the enemy. Maximum weight 1,415 lb; span 26 feet 6 inches. *"Flight" photo. (top right)*

## 1916: Supermarine Night Hawk

The first aircraft to bear the name Supermarine, intended primarily for anti-Zeppelin patrols and designed to cruise economically at very low speeds. The armament was one $1\frac{1}{2}$-pounder gun and single machine guns fore and aft. Equipment included a sleeping berth in the enclosed crew compartment and a searchlight fed by a motorcycle engine and generator. With two 100hp Anzani engines the aircraft is reputed to have flown satisfactorily. Maximum weight 6,146 lb; span 60 feet. *Imperial War Museum photo.*
*(centre right)*

## 1916: Armstrong Whitworth FK8

The second Armstrong Whitworth aircraft to go into production was the FK8, a solidly built biplane with a Beardmore engine. It served in large numbers as a reconnaisance and bombing aircraft both in France, where two FK8 pilots won the VC, and in the Middle East. After the war a civil FK8 owned by Qantas had the distinction of operating Australia's first air mail service on November 2, 1922, between Clareville and Cloncurry. Maximum weight 2,800 lb; span 43 feet 6 inches.
*(bottom right)*

**1916: Vickers FB14**

A single-seat, general purpose, tractor biplane, the forerunner of a long line of Vickers tractor biplanes. The prototype was initially fitted with a 160 hp Beardmore engine in place of the intended 200hp and was therefore underpowered. The type was used in small quantities but only a few ever received suitable engines although both the Rolls-Royce Eagle and the RAF 4a were used. Maximum weight 2,603 lb; span 39 feet 6 inches. *(left)*

**1916: Bristol M1C**

This aeroplane had the distinction of being the only British monoplane fighter to be produced during the 1914-18 war. Powered by a 110hp Le Rhone rotary engine, the M1C had a top speed of 130 mph with excellent handling qualities. Unfortunately, a landing speed of nearly 50 mph and the official prejudice against monoplanes meant that this aircraft was built only in small numbers and its operations were confined to the Middle East theatre. Maximum weight 1,350 lb; span 30 feet 9 inches. *(above)*

**1916: de Havilland DH5**

Unconventional in appearance, the DH5 was, at first, viewed with suspicion by pilots. The back-stagger configuration was adopted in order to provide a view comparable to that of the pusher scout. In fact, the DH5, with its Le Rhone or Clerget rotary engine, was easy to fly but its performance fell off above 10,000 feet; it was, however, used to good effect for low-level ground attack on the Western Front. Maximum weight 1,490 lb; span 25 feet 8 inches. *(above left)*

### 1916: Armstrong Whitworth FK10 Quadruplane

The success of the Triplane led to a large number of triplane designs, both Allied and German, but quadruplanes were not so common: one of the few, the FK10, was built by Armstrong Whitworth. It was intended to be a two-seat fighter and was fitted with either a Clerget or a Le Rhone rotary engine. The performance proved to be disappointing and only a small number of FK10s were built. Maximum weight 2,020 lb; span 27 feet 10 inches. *Imperial War Museum photo. (left)*

### 1916: de Havilland DH4

The DH4 day bomber was the most successful of the wartime de Havilland aircraft. The first DH4s were fitted with the BHP engine, the forerunner of the Armstrong Siddeley Puma, but a variety of other engines were fitted, including the Rolls-Royce Eagle of 375hp. with this engine it could fly faster than the contemporary fighters. The DH4 was adopted by the U.S. Army and was built in large numbers in America. Maximum weight 3,470 lb; span 42 feet 5 inches. *(left)*

### 1916: Bristol F2B Fighter

Powered by a 275hp Rolls-Royce Falcon engine, it was one of the most successful two-seat fighters of the 1914-18 war; fast and manoeuvrable, with the pilot and observer placed close together, each with his own guns, the Bristol Fighter proved to be a formidable opponent. It was built in large numbers and production continued until 1926. In an army-cooperation role the "Brisfit" served with the R.A.F. until 1932. Maximum weight 2,800 lb; span 39 feet 3 inches. *"Flight" photo. (above)*

### 1917: F.B. 26 Vampire

With their last fighter of the 1914-18 war, Vickers reverted to the single-seat pusher layout; the F.B. 26 Vampire was powered by a 200hp Hispano-Suiza engine, but the F.B. 26A, an armoured version for trench strafing, had a 200 hp Bentley BR2 rotary engine. This version, which was fitted with two nose-mounted Lewis guns, had a top speed of 130 mph. Three Vampires were built, but the type did not go into production. Maximum weight (F.B. 26A) 2,438 lb; span 31 feet 6 inches. *Imperial War Museum photo. (right)*

above the top wing and the landing speed rather high, it was, at first, disliked by some pilots. It nevertheless gave a good account of itself and was notable as being the first British multi-gun fighter, having an armament of four machine guns The Dolphin Mk 1 was powered by a 200hp Hispano Suiza engine. Maximum weight 2,000 lb; span 32 feet 6 inches. *(below left)*

### 1917: Sopwith Cuckoo
The first aeroplane to be built as a torpedo-carrier for operation from an aircraft carrier. Early production Cuckoos were, in fact, made by Blackburns, Sopwith being at the time pre-occupied with other types, but difficulties with the Sunbeam Arab engines prevented the aircraft from playing any part in the war. Later with a Wolseley Viper engine, the Cuckoo gave good service embarked in the carriers *HMS Furious and Eagle.* Maximum weight 3,875 lb; span 46 feet 9 inches. *Imperial War Museum photo. (left)*

### 1917: Bristol MR 1 Biplane
An early example of all-metal construction, the Bristol MR 1 biplane was designed to forestall a possible shortage of aircraft timber. The MR 1 had a semi-monocoque fuselage with a smooth duralumin skin riveted to an inner corrugated skin. The first aircraft had wooden wings but the second had fabric covered steel wings. The aircraft performed well with a 180hp Wolseley Viper engine but was not put into production. Maximum weight 2,810 lb; span 42 feet 2 inches. *(left)*

### 1916: Sopwith Camel
Perhaps the most famous fighter of the First World War, the Sopwith Camel served with the R.F.C., and R.N.A.S. and the R.A.F. from the middle of 1917 until the war's end. Tricky to fly, it was, nevertheless, a superb fighting machine and was responsible for destroying 1,294 enemy aircraft, more than any other single type. Among a multitude of notable exploits was the shooting down of the German ace von Richtofen in April 1918. Maximum weight 1,480 lb; span 28 feet. *(right)*

### 1917: Vickers FB16D
During the 1914-18 war Vickers produced a series of fighter designs, some of which saw active service in small numbers. The best of these was the FB16D, originally designed for the ill-fated Hart radial engine but eventually emerging with a 200hp Hispano Suiza. The FB16D was flown by the British ace Major McCudden who claimed that at 10,000 feet it was

30 mph faster than anything he had previously flown. The FB16D was, however, not put into production. Maximum weight 1,775 lb; span 25 feet. *(above top)*

### 1917: Sopwith Dolphin
In appearance the Dolphin represented a departure from the Sopwith tradition, and because the pilot's head was exposed

## 1917: Sopwith Snipe

The advent of the 230hp Bentley rotary engine, the BR2, led to the production of the Snipe, the last Sopwith to go into action and virtually the last of the rotary-engined fighters. The war finished before the Snipe could play a decisive part but it will always be remembered for the single-handed combat fought against great odds by Major Barker in October 1918, for which he was awarded the VC. Maximum weight 2,020 lb; span 31 feet 1 inch. *(left)*

### 1917: Vickers Vimy

The best of the British bombers of the 1914-18 war, was designed, built and tested all within five months. The third prototype, and the first production batch, had 300hp Fiat engines, but the majority

were fitted with 360hp Rolls-Royce Eagles. The Vimy was just too late for the war, but a Vimy flown by Alcock and Brown achieved fame by being the first aircraft to fly non-stop across the Atlantic. Maximum weight 12,500 lb; span 68 feet. *Imperial War Museum photo.* *(top right)*

### 1917: de Havilland DH9A

The DH9, introduced as a DH4 replacement and used in large numbers towards the end of the war, proved to be underpowered and something of a disappointment, but the DH9A, pictured above, with the 400hp Liberty engine then becoming available from the United States was, by contrast, outstandingly successful. Used to bomb

Germany during the closing stages of the war, it remained the standard day bomber—and maid-of-all-work—with the R.A.F. until 1931. Maximum weight (DH9A) 4,650 lb; span 45 feet 11 inches. *(above centre)*

### 1917: Blackburn Kangaroo

With two 250hp Rolls-Royce Falcon engines, this aeroplane was used for patrol duties over the North Sea. At first it was built with unsprung undercarriages, a feature soon to be modified. In 1919 a Kangaroo entered the race to Australia but retired in Crete. Two other competed in the 1922 King's Cup Race and three, known as Pip, Squeak and Wilfred, served with the Blackburn Flying School until

1929. Maximum weight 8,500 lb; span 74 feet 10 inches. *(bottom far right)*

### 1918: Supermarine Baby

Fitted with a 200hp Hispano-

Suiza engine, it was Britain's
first single-seat fighter flying
boat. With a top speed of
117 mph, the Baby had a
performance and
manoeuvrability which compared
well with contemporary
landplane fighters, but it did not
go into production. The Baby,
which had folding wings, was
the forerunner of other
Supermarine fighter boats and
of the successful Schneider
Trophy Sea Lion racers.
Maximum weight 2,326 lb; span
30 feet 6 inches. *Imperial War
Museum photo. (top far left)*

### 1918: English Electric Phoenix P5 Cork Flying Boat

With a monocoque hull having
two layers of diagonal
mahagony planking, it marked a
significant advance in flying
boat design. Three were built,
two having two Rolls-Royce
engines while the Mk III had
450hp Napier Lions. The MK II
had gunner nacelles mounted
outboard under the trailing edge
of the upper wing. The Cork
was successful but production
was cancelled at the end of the
war. Maximum weight 12,500 lb;
span 85 feet. *Imperial War
Museum photo. (top right)*

### 1918: Bristol Scout F

A promising single-seat fighter
was the Bristol Scout F. Too late
to take part in the war, the
Scout F was originally powered
by a 200hp Sunbeam Arab, but
the engine suffered from
incurable vibration. The third
Scout, known as the F1, was
fitted with the new 315hp
Cosmos Mercury engine. Thus
powered it had a speed of
145 mph and climbed 10,000 feet
in 5½ minutes. Maximum weight
2,260 lb; span 29 feet 7 inches.
*(second from top)*

### 1918: Bristol Braemar

The imposing Braemar arrived
too late to take part in the war
but subsequently two other
versions were built, the Tramp,
with a central engine room and
shaft drive to the propellers, and
the Pullman, with an enclosed
cabin for 14 passengers. The
Pullman flew successfully but
was not put into commercial
service. The Braemar, with four
400hp Liberty engines,
performed well, having a top
speed of 125 mph. Maximum
weight (Braemar) 18,000 lb; span
81 feet 8 inches. *(bottom left)*

### 1918: de Havilland DH10A

Designed as a high-speed day
bomber, the DH10A, with two
400hp Liberty engines, appeared
just too late for the war but,
given a chance, it would have
proved an effective weapon; it
could carry 1,000 lb of bombs
with fuel for 700 miles and its
speed was not far short of
contemporary fighters. Big
production orders were cancelled
at the end of the war and the
DH10 found no place in civil
aviation. Maximum weight
9,457 lb; span 65 feet 6 inches.
*(below left)*

### 1918: Armstrong Whitworth Ara

The last aeroplane to be
produced by Armstrong
Whitworth at Newcastle on Tyne
before they closed down their
aircraft department in 1919. The
Ara fighter was a two-bay
biplane designed for the 320hp
ABC Dragonfly radial engine.
The Ara had a good
performance but, like numerous
other excellent aircraft which
emerged at the end of the war, it
suffered eclipse because of the
failure of the engine. Maximum
weight 1,930 lb; span 27 feet
5 inches. *(left)*

# BETWEEN THE WARS

### 1919: Pemberton Billing Supermarine Channel

The Channel civil flying boat was a modification of the Admiralty-designed AD flying boat built by the Pemberton Billing company. Converted to carry three passengers, the Channels were mostly fitted with a 160hp Beardmore engine, although the Mk II had a 240hp Siddeley Puma. Channel boats gave joyrides at seaside resorts during 1919 and later inaugurated the world's first international flying boat service, between Southampton and Le Havre. Maximum weight (Mk II) 3,700 lb; span 50 feet 6 inches. *Imperial War Museum photo. (right)*

### 1919: de Havilland DH16

After the war both the DH4 and the DH9A were converted for passenger carrying and were used on the continental services operated by Aircraft Transport and Travel Ltd. The DH16, pictured below, was a DH9A modified to take four passengers and fitted with Rolls-Royce Eagle engines. The DH4A was similar in appearance but carried only two passengers. A DH16 was used by KLM to inaugurate its schedule service between Amsterdam and London. Maximum weight (DH16) 4,470 lb; span 46 feet 6 inches. *(below)*

### 1919: Vickers Vimy Commercial

Vickers, anxious to exploit the qualities of the Vimy, quickly produced a civil transport version. Known as the Vimy Commercial, it had the wings, tail assembly, powerplants and undercarriages of the bomber with a new fuselage capable of seating ten passengers in a comfortable cabin. Forty Vimy Commercials were sold to China, one went to France and another to Russia. Most famous of all was the *City of London* which operated with Instone Air Line and Imperial Airways until 1926. Maximum weight 12,500 lb; span 68 feet. *"Flight" photo. (above)*

### 1919: Sopwith Atlantic

Built to compete for the £10,000 *Daily Mail* prize for the first non-stop Atlantic flight, the Sopwith Atlantic had a boat built into the fuselage decking, a jettisonable undercarriage, fuel for 22 hours and a Rolls-Royce Eagle engine. Hawker and his navigator left Newfoundland on May 8, 1919; nothing more was heard from them until a week later when news was received that they had been rescued by a ship without radio. Maximum weight 6,150 lb; span 46 feet 6 inches. *(left)*

### 1919: Bristol Badger F2C

Designed as a 2-seat fighter-reconnaissance biplane. Too late for the war, the Badger had the distinction of taking the first Cosmos Jupiter nine-cylinder, radial engine on its first flight. Later, in 1920, the Cosmos assets were acquired by Bristols and the Bristol Jupiter engine became the most successful air-cooled British engine of the early 1930s, being manufactured in at least 17 overseas countries. Maximum weight 6,150 lb; span 36 feet 9 inches. *(right)*

### 1919: Avro Baby

One of the first post-war attempts to produce a "sporting" aeroplane. Fitted with a 35hp Green water-cooled engine, it quickly distinguished itself by winning the handicap section of the 1919 Aerial Derby at 70·3 mph. Later in 1920, it was flown by Bert Hinckler non-stop from Croydon to Turin in $9\frac{1}{2}$ hours. Several variants of the Baby were built but there was no large-scale production. Maximum weight (approx) 850 lb; span 25 feet. *"Flight" photo. (right)*

### 1919: Sopwith Gnu

One of the first aircraft to appear with an enclosed passenger cabin after the war, powered by a 110hp Le Rhone rotary engine. The Gnu went into limited production and saw some service with airlines in Australia; others were used for joy-riding in the United Kingdom. The prototype Gnu appeared at Hendon in May 1919 as the second aircraft on the newly-introduced British civil register, bearing the marks K-101. Maximum weight 3,300 lb; span 38 feet 1 inch. *(right)*

### 1919: Vickers Viking Mk III

One of 31 Viking amphibian flying boat variants built between 1919 and 1923. The aircraft illustrated won the first prize of £10,000 in the Air Ministry Commercial Amphibian Competition held in 1920. In 1921 G-EAUK flew a series of experimental services between the River Thames in London and the River Seine in Paris, a journey which took some $2\frac{1}{4}$ hours. Maximum weight (GHEAUK) 4,545 lb; span 46 feet. *(below)*

### 1919: Sopwith Wallaby

After the war the Australian Government offered a prize of £10,000 for the first England-Australia flight, and Sopwith built a modified version of the Atlantic biplane known as the Wallaby. It had a Rolls-Royce Eagle engine and carried 200 gallons of fuel, enough for 1,500 miles. The Wallaby's flight to Australia ended when the aircraft was damaged at Bali, but it was subsequently repaired and used as an eight-seater on the Adelaide-Sydney route. Maximum weight 5,200 lb; span 46 feet 6 inches. *(below)*

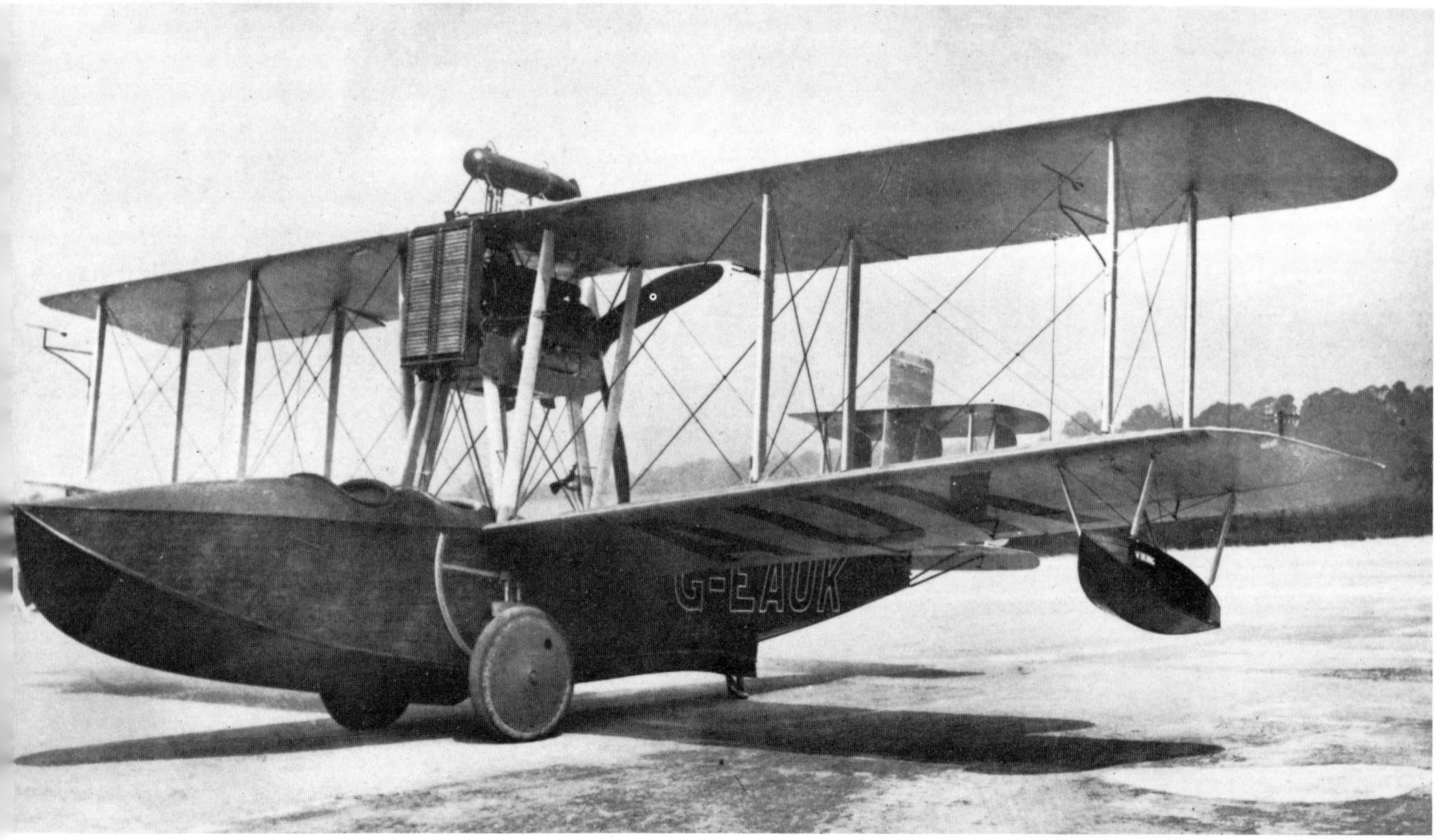

**1920: Avro 547 Triplane**

For its first commercial aircraft Avro reverted to the triplane layout with the Type 547. Apart from a specially-built fuselage with a cabin for four passengers and the 160hp Beardmore engine, the 547 was built up almost entirely of Avro 504K parts. The Triplane was entered for the Air Ministry Small Commercial Aeroplane Competition in 1920, but it failed to qualify for an award and, as it proved to be somewhat heavy and slow, it was not further developed. Maximum weight 3,800 lb; span 37 feet 3 inches. *(top right)*

**1920: de Havilland DH 18**

The first de Havilland aircraft to be designed from the start as an airliner; it also bridged the gap in 1920 between the closing of the Aircraft Manufacturing Company and the formation of the de Havilland Aircraft Company at Stag Lane Aerodrome. With a Napier Lion engine of 450hp the DH 18 carried eight passengers (and at one stage a cabin boy) and marked a significant step forward in operating economy. Maximum weight 7,450 lb; span 51 feet 3 inches. *(above right)*

**1920: Bristol Bullet Racer**

Built mainly to provide a test bed for the Cosmos (later Bristol) Jupiter engine. Only one was built but during its life it was extremely modified. It originated with comparatively large wings; later it appeared with a much deeper fuselage. It competed in several King's Cup races and, in its final form with a much reduced span, it achieved a speed of 170 mph. Maximum weight 2,300 lb; span 22 feet 4 inches. *(above right)*

**1920: Sopwith Antelope**

Exhibited at the 1920 Aero Show at Olympia and subsequently entered for the Air Ministry Small Commercial Aeroplane Competition in which it won second place and a £3,000 prize. Powered by a 180hp Wolseley Viper, the Antelope had a small cabin for two passengers immediately behind the pilot. After the competition the Antelope was shipped to Australia where it was employed on the southern air mail routes. Maximum weight 3,000 lb; span 46 feet 6 inches. *(right)*

### 1920: Supermarine Amphibian

The Amphibian was built for the Air Ministry Commercial Amphibian Competition held at Martlesham Heath and Felixstowe in 1920. Powered by a 360hp Rolls-Royce Eagle engine, the Amphibian housed two passengers in an enclosed cabin ahead of the pilot. The land undercarriage was retractable sideways into position under the wing. The result of the competition was a close finish between the winning Vickers Viking and the Supermarine. Maximum weight 5,700 lb; span 50 feet. *"Flight" photo. (above right)*

### 1921: Bristol Ten-Seater

The first Bristol commercial to be designed as such was the Ten-Seater which, with a 450hp Napier Lion engine carried two pilots and eight passengers. The first aircraft, G-EAWY, was used briefly by Instone Airline and Handley Page Transport. Two similar machines were built, both with 450hp Jupiter engines; G-EBEV served as a freighter with Instone Airline and Imperial Airways, the other being completed as an ambulance for the R.A.F. and called Brandon. Maximum weight (G-EAWY) 6,800 lb; span 54 feet 3 inches. *(above right)*

### 1921: Avro Bison

Designed to a restrictive specification as a deck-landing, fleet spotter-reconnaissance aircraft, the Bison was ugly but effective. Early examples had claws on the axle to catch the wires on the carrier's decks

which then ran fore-and-aft and not athwartships as is the modern way. The Avro Bison, powered by a 450hp Naper Lion engine, served with both the R.A.F. and the Fleet Air Arm from 1922 to 1929. Maximum weight 6,130 lb; span 46 feet *(left)*

### 1921: Gloster Mars 1

The first Gloster-designed aircraft was a racing biplane known officially as the Mars I but unofficially, and universally, as the "Bamel". Built in two months and fitted with a 450hp Napier Lion engine, it won the 1921 Aerial Derby at 163 mph; subsequently it was timed over a measured course at an average speed of 212 mph. The Mars I "Bamel" was the forerunner of a notable line of Folland-designed racing aircraft. Maximum weight 2,500 lb; span 23 feet. *"Flight" photo. (left)*

### 1921: Blackburn Dart

The Dart, the first of a long line of Blackburn torpedo-bombers to go into production, served with the Royal Navy from 1924 until it was replaced by another Blackburn aircraft in 1933. The first deck-landing trials were carried out in 1921 on *H.M.S. Argus* and later, in 1926, a Dart made the first night landing on the deck of a carrier. The engine was a 450hp Napier Lion. Maximum weight 6,300 lb; span 45 feet 6 inches. *(top centre)*

### 1922: Avro Aldershot

A single-engined bomber designed around the new 650hp Rolls-Royce Condor engine. The fuselage was divided into two storeys with the pilot and gunner above and the bomber and W/T operator below. An ambulance version built in 1924 was called the Andover. One Aldershot was used as a flying test-bed for both the 16-cylinder 1,000hp Napier Cub engine and for the 850hp six-cylinder inverted Beardmore Typhoon. Maximum weight 10,950 lb; span 68 feet. *(top right)*

### 1922: de Havilland DH 34

Another step forward in operating economy, able to carry ten passengers with a 450hp Napier Lion, the same engine as its predecessor the DH 18. The DH 34 had a relatively high wing loading and was at first criticised for its high landing speed of about 70 mph. The

aircraft served with the pioneer airlines on routes from London to Paris, Brussels, Cologne, Amsterdam and Berlin until withdrawn in 1926. Maximum weight 7,200 lb; span 51 feet 4 inches. *(below centre)*

### 1922: Vickers Vulcan

An attempt to produce a highly economical transport capable of paying its way without a subsidy. With eight passengers and a 360hp Rolls-Royce Eagle engine, the aircraft proved to be underpowered and its performance was disappointing. The Vulcan was, however, used in small numbers by Instone Airline and by Imperial Airways, and later examples with Napier Lion engines remained in service until 1928. Maximum weight (Rolls-Royce) 6,150 lb; span 49 feet. *(below left)*

### 1922: Blackburn Fleet Reconnaissance-Spotter Mk II

A somewhat portly biplane, the Blackburn served alongside the Blackburn Dart in the Royal Navy during the 1920s. The Mk II, illustrated above, first embarked in *H.M.S. Furious* in 1926. In addition to the pilot the Blackburn carried in its commodious cabin a navigator-observer and a telegraphist-air gunner. Not declared obsolete until 1933, it was fitted with a 450hp Napier Lion engine. Maximum weight 5,960 lb; span 45 feet 6 inches. *(below)*

### 1922: Vickers Virginia

The mainstay of the R.A.F.'s heavy night-bomber force from 1924 until 1937, and some were still operating as parachute trainers as late as 1941. The prototype had its 450hp Napier Lion engines mounted on the lower wing but production aircraft had nacelles raised above the wing. A total of 126 Virginias was built in seven different marks, the Mk X, with 50 aircraft being the most numerous variant. Maximum weight (Mk X) 17,600 lb; span 87 feet 8 inches. *(above)*

### 1922: Vickers Victoria

Based on the Virginia bomber, the Victoria replaced the Vernon as the R.A.F.'s troop carrier. Most Victorias were powered by Napier Lion engines but the Mk IV illustrated had 660hp Bristol Pegasus radials. The Victoria made R.A.F. history by taking part in the evacuation of Kabul, in Afghanistan, during the riots of 1928-29, when they helped to rescue 586 civilians. The Victoria was replaced by the similar Valentia, some of which served until 1943. Maximum weight (Mk IV) 17,600 lb; span 87 feet 4 inches. *(below)*

### 1922: Supermarine Seagull

A tractor, amphibian flying boat, the Seagull was designed for deck landing and naval reconnaissance duties. Carrying a crew of three, the Seagull was powered by a 450hp Napier Lion engine and had a retractable landing chassis. A small batch of Seagulls worked with the R.A.F. and six served with the Royal Australian Air Force. Some of these formed a special flight which undertook a photographic survey of the Great Barrier Reef. Maximum weight 5,869 lb; span 46 feet. *Imperial War Museum photo. (opposite page top)*

### 1922: Supermarine Sea Lion II

Winner of the Schneider Trophy race at Naples in 1922, this was a modified version of the Sea King II, a single-seat, amphibian fighter. The modifications included removing the amphibian gear, reducing the span by four feet and fitting a 450hp Napier Lion engines in place of the 300hp Hispano-Suiza engine. The Sea Lion completed the 230-mile course at an average speed of 135·7 mph. Maximum weight 3,163 lb; span 28 feet. *"Flight" photo. (opposite page top right)*

## 1922: Bristol Type 72 Monoplane

Of the several racing aeroplanes built by Bristol to develop and publicise the Jupiter engine, none showed more originality than the Type 72. With its small cantilever wings, retractable undercarriage and totally enclosed engine, the design was well ahead of its time. On its first flight, wing flexing led to instability; this was cured by the addition of external bracing wires, but later spinner trouble prevented the machine from showing its full potential and development was abandoned. Span 25 feet 2 inches. *(above right)*

## 1923: Vickers Vixen

The Vixen was the first of a family of two-seat, fighter-reconnaissance-bomber aircraft produced by Vickers which carried various names including Valparaiso, Venture, Vivid and Valiant and which were mostly powered by Napier Lion engines. Six Ventures were supplied to the R.A.F. but the principal customer was Portugal which purchased 14 Valparaisos and built at least 13 more under licence. Chile also bought 18 Vixen Mk Vs and the prototype Valiant. Maximum weight (Vixen) 4,720 lb; Span 40 feet. *(above right)*

## 1923: Bristol Taxiplane and Primary Trainer

A little known but successful Bristol aircraft, powered by the 140hp Bristol Lucifer engine. The three-seat Taxiplane proved to be underpowered, but the two-seat Trainer had a good performance and nine of the type were used by the Bristol R.A.F. Reserve Flying School; some of them remained in service until replaced by de Havilland Tiger Moths in 1932. In addition, 12 Trainers were sold to Chile and three went to Hungary. Maximum weight 1,900 lb; span 31 feet 1 inch. *(above right)*

## 1922: Armstrong Whitworth Siskin

The Siskin III and IIIA were the mainstay of the R.A.F.'s fighter force during the 1920s and the early 1930s. The Siskin had its origin in a fighter built by the Siddeley Deasy company and fitted with the unsuccessful ABC Dragonfly engine. It was not until the appearance in 1922 of the Armstrong Siddeley Jaguar powerplant, that the developed Siskin, the R.A.F.'s first all-metal aircraft, became a reality. Maximum weight 3,010 lb; span 33 feet 2 inches. *(below)*

### 1923: English Electric Wren

This ultra-light aircraft was built for the Light Aeroplane Competition held in 1923. The Wren flew strongly, powered by a twin-cylinder motorcycle engine of 398 c.c. which developed 6hp at 2,750 rpm. With a wing loading of $2\frac{3}{4}$ lb per square foot, it took off in 50 yards and had a speed range of 23 to 52 mph. During the trials the Wren flew a distance of 87·5 miles on one imperial gallon of fuel. Maximum weight 420 lb; span 37 feet. *"Flight" photo. (above)*

### 1923: Bristol Bullfinch

Powered by a 425hp Bristol Jupiter engine, it was a novel design for a single-seat monoplane fighter which could be readily converted into a two-seat reconnaissance biplane. The alteration was brought about by inserting, behind the pilot's cockpit, an extra fuselage section containing the gunner's cockpit and carrying a cantilever bottom wing. The monoplane had a good performance but the biplane was overweight and could not carry its prescribed military load. Maximum weight (monoplane) 3,205 lb; span 18 feet 6 inches. *(top centre)*

### 1923: Bristol Bloodhound

Intended to replace the Bristol F2B Fighter, a civil prototype G-EBGG, and three others for the R.A.F. were built but there was no production order. The Bloodhound's main contribution was to establish the integrity of the Bristol Jupiter engine. In 1925 G-EBGG flew an extended trial with a sealed engine, covering 25,074 miles with the engine seals unbroken. Later, it flew to Cairo and back in 56 hours. Maximum weight 4,236 lb; span 40 feet 2 inches. *(top right)*

### 1923: Hawker Woodcock

The first Hawker aeroplane to go into production and the first of the firm's long line of fighters, the Woodcock became the R.A.F.'s standard night-fighter. As first flown the Woodcock proved unsatisfactory, but with redesigned wings, modified tail surfaces and a Bristol Jupiter engine in place of the original Armstrong Siddeley Jaguar, the aircraft became popular with pilots and some Woodcocks were still flying with the R.A.F. as late as 1936. Maximum weight 2,980 lb; span 32 feet 6 inches. *(right centre)*

### 1923: Supermarine Sea Eagle

This amphibian flying boat was built for the Southampton-Guernsey service started in 1923 by the British Marine Air Navigation Company, which was later absorbed by Imperial Airways. The Sea Eagle carried six passengers in a cabin in the forepart of the hull and was initially fitted with a 360hp Rolls-Royce Eagle engine, later replaced by a 450hp Napier Lion. The Guernsey service ceased in 1929 and the Sea Eagles were scrapped. Maximum weight 6,050 lb; span 46 feet. *(right)*

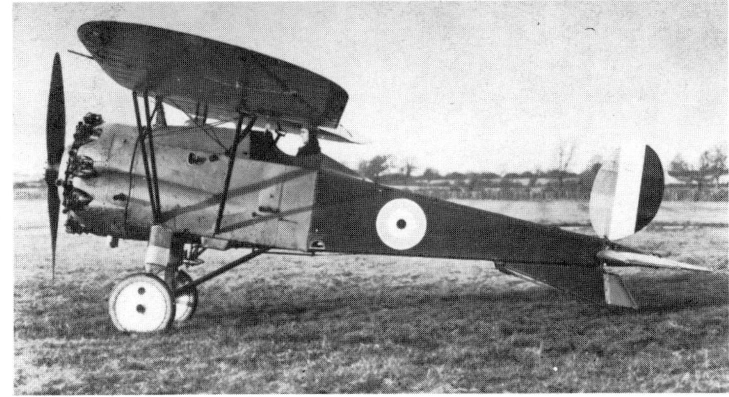

### 1923: Gloster Grebe

The Gloster company's first fighter to go into large-scale production; it was powered by an Armstrong Siddeley Jaguar engine of 350hp and it served with the R.A.F. until 1931. In 1926 two Grebes were launched experimentally from the airship R33 (built by Armstrong Whitworth) and in 1929 a two-seat version, flown by Richard Atcherley, won the King's Cup race at an average speed of 150 mph. Maximum weight 2,600 lb; span 29 feet 4 inches. *(right)*

### 1923: De Havilland DH50

Designed as a light transport and as a replacement for the civilianised DH9, much used for charter and taxi work, the DH50 carried four passengers and was powered by a 230hp Armstrong Siddeley Puma engine. It found favour especially abroad and was manufactured under licence in Australia, Belgium and Czechoslovakia. A DH50J fitted with an Armstrong Siddeley Jaguar engine, pictured above, was used by Alan Cobham on his flights to Cape Town and Australia. Maximum weight (Puma) 3,900 lb; span 42 feet 9 inches. *"Flight" photo. (right centre)*

### 1924: English Electric M3 Ayr

An experimental aircraft designated as a coastal patrol flying boat. Its main feature was the use of buoyant sponsons, in the form of stub wings, to give lateral stability on the water, the object being to eliminate the normal wing-tip floats, always the flying boat's most vulnerable element. Powered by a 450hp Napier Lion engine, the three-seat Ayr had a good performance but was not ordered into production. Span 46 feet. *Imperial War Museum photo. (right)*

### 1924: Supermarine Scarab

This naval reconnaissance bomber amphibian flying boat was the subject of a substantial order from the Spanish government who used it with considerable success in operations in Morocco during 1924. The crew of three was seated ahead of the wings with the pilot in front, the gunner close behind and the navigator behind him. The Scarab was powered by a 360hp Rolls-Royce Eagle engine and could carry 1,000 lb of bombs. Maximum weight 5,750 lb; span 46 feet. *(right)*

### 1924: Avro 504N

After many modifications and tests, the ultimate development of the Avro 504 formula, the 504N, pictured above, continued to be the R.A.F.'s primary trainer until 1933. The type was also used by the air forces of Belgium, Brazil, Chile, Denmark, Greece, Japan, South Africa, Thailand and Sweden. After disposal by the Air Ministry many 504Ns went on to the civil register. The engine was a 180hp Armstrong Siddeley Lynx. Maximum weight 2,240 lb; span 36 feet. *(above)*

### 1924: Blackburn Cubaroo

One of the biggest single-engine aeroplanes of its time, the Cubaroo was built to take the new Napier Cub, a 16-cylinder water-cooled X-shaped engine developing 1,000hp. The Cubaroo, which could lift a payload of $3\frac{1}{2}$ tons, did not go into production but two were built, one subsequently being used as a flying test-bed for another experimental engine, the 1,000 hp Beardmore Simoon. Maximum weight 19,000 lb; span 88 feet. *(above)*

### 1924: Bristol Brownie

Designed for the 1924 Air Ministry Two-Seat, Light Aeroplane Competition for aircraft with engines not exceeding 1,100 c.c. Three Brownies were built, all with Bristol Cherub 32hp, twin-cylinder engines of 1,095 c.c. The Brownie won second place but, like all the entrants, proved to be too fragile and underpowered for the proposed government-sponsored light aeroplane clubs. Maximum weight 870 lb; span 36 feet 7 inches. *(above right)*

### 1924: English Electric Kingston

This flying boat was a development of the successful P5 Cork aircraft of 1918. The first version, like the Cork, had a double-skin, wooden monocoque hull but a second aircraft, which appeared about a year later, had a metal hull. The Kingston was a five-seat reconnaissance aircraft and both versions had two 450hp Napier Lion engines, the nacelles of which were extended rearwards to house a gunner's cockpit. Maximum weight 14,117 lb; span 85 feet 6 inches. *Imperial War Museum photo. (right)*

### 1924: Supermarine Sparrow

A biplane built for the Air Ministry Two-Seat Light Aeroplane Competition of 1924. It was powered by a Blackburn 3-cylinder, radial engine which failed before the aircraft could compete. Rebuilt with a parasol monoplane wing and a Bristol Cherub engine, for the 1926 Lympne Light Aeroplane Trials, the Sparrow II was again eliminated after a forced landing. It was, however, subsequently used with success by the Halton Aero Club. Maximum weight (Sparrow II) 1,000 lb; span 34 feet. *(above)*

**1924: Supermarine Swan**

A twin-engine, amphibian flying boat, the Swan was built for the Air Ministry and was originally powered by two 360hp Rolls-Royce Eagle engines. Later, a civil version was produced accommodating ten passengers and powered by two 450hp Napier Lion engines. This aircraft was operated experimentally by Imperial Airways in 1927. The Swan formed the basis for the highly successful Southampton flying boat. Maximum weight (Napier Lion) 13,710 lb; span 69 feet. *Imperial War Museum photo. (top right)*

**1924: Blackburn Bluebird**

The first Bluebird was built for the light aeroplane competition of 1924, but the first production model, the Bluebird II appeared in 1927 with a 60hp Armstrong Siddeley Genet engine. Later versions, the Mk III and the Mk IV, both fitted with a variety of air-cooled engines, were built in considerable numbers. The Bluebird was unusual among contemporary light aircraft in that the two occupants sat side-by-side. Maximum weight (Mk IV) 1,640 lb; span 30 feet *(right)*

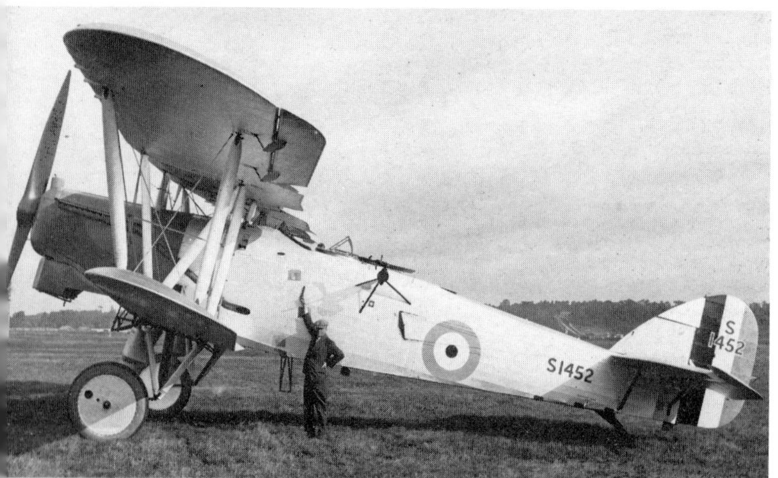

### 1925: Hawker Horsley

A torpedo bomber with a Rolls-Royce Condor engine of 650hp, built for the R.A.F. during a transition period at Hawkers, the first Horsleys being of wooden construction and the later ones of metal. In 1927 an R.A.F. Horsley attempted to fly non-stop to India but was forced down in the Persian Gulf. It nevertheless succeeded in breaking the world's long-distance record, having flown 3,240 miles. Maximum weight 7,800 lb; span 56 feet 6 inches. *(left)*

### 1925: de Havilland DH60 Moth

The very light aeroplanes fostered by the competition were not entirely satisfactory and Geoffrey de Havilland put his own ideas into the DH60 Moth, an aircraft which proved to be ideal for flying clubs and the private owner. The Moth sold in large numbers all over the world and it made many long-distance record flights. By 1929 Moths, costing £650 complete, were coming off the line at the rate of nearly one a day. Maximum weight (DH60G) 1,650 lb; span 30 feet. *(above)*

### 1925: Gloster Gamecock

The Gamecock followed the Grebe, and was the last fighter of wooden construction to be ordered for the R.A.F., it was introduced in 1926 and remained in service until 1931. Gamecocks gave many memorable displays of aerobatics at the R.A.F. Pageants and they won the squadron race for the Sassoon Cup three years running, the last in 1929 at a speed of 156 mph. Maximum weight 2,850 ft; span 29 feet 10 inches. *"Flight" photo. (centre left)*

### 1925: Armstrong Whitworth Atlas

The R.A.F.'s standard army cooperation aircraft from 1927, and it continued to serve as an advanced trainer until 1925. Some Atlases supplied to the Royal Canadian Air Force were still operational at the outbreak of war in 1939. The Atlas had a 450hp Armstrong Siddeley Jaguar—and a hook which could be lowered to pick up messages. Maximum weight 4,020 lb; span 39 feet 7 inches. *(opposite page bottom)*

### 1925: Supermarine S4

Supermarine's aircraft for the 1925 Schneider Trophy contest held in the USA was the S4, a clean, cantilever-wing monoplane powered by a 700hp Napier Lion engine. Unfortunately, the S4 crashed into the sea off a steep turn during the navigability trials and was wrecked, the pilot surviving. Before that it had achieved an average speed of 226·8 mph over a 3 km course, thus regaining for Britain the World Speed Record. Maximum weight 3,192 lb; span 30 feet 8 inches. *(top right)*

### 1925: Supermarine Southampton

With two Napier Lion Engines, this aircraft marked an important step forward in flying boat design. The first Southamptons had wooden hulls but the Mk II boats with metal hulls were 540 lb lighter. R.A.F. Southamptons, which served for more than a decade, made several historic flights, culminating in 1927 in a 27,000-mile cruise by four aircraft from England to Australia, round that continent and back to Singapore. Maximum weight 15,200 lb; span 75 feet. *Imperial War Museum photo. (right)*

### 1925: Gloster III

A racing seaplane, two of which were built for the 1925 Schneider Trophy race held that year of which one came second to the Americans, having lapped at 199 mph. Both aircraft, which were fitted with special Napier Lion engines developing 670hp, were re-built and used as practice aircraft by the R.A.F. teams that participated in subsequent Schneider Trophy races. Maximum weight 2,690 lb; span 20 feet. *(right)*

### 1925: Vickers Vespa

This biplane was built as a private venture for army cooperation duties and was powered by a 455hp Bristol Jupiter engine. In 1929 six Vespas were delivered to the Bolivian Army and later four were supplied to the Irish Free State. The Vespa had a good climb performance and a specially modified Mk IV, with a supercharged Bristol Pegasus engine, captured the World's Altitude Record by reaching 43,976 feet in September 1932. Maximum weight 4,370 lb; span 50 feet. *Imperial War Museum photo. (top left)*

### 1926: Armstrong Whitworth Argosy

Their first civil aircraft carrying 20 passengers and fitted with three Armstrong Siddeley Jaguar engines. Serving with Imperial Airways, the Argosy introduced the "Silver Wing" luxury service between London and Paris; it also flew the first stage of the India service started in 1929. Later Argosies were used on the Cairo-Khartoum section of the African route and one was still giving joyrides at Blackpool in 1936. Maximum weight 19,200 lb; span 90 feet 4 inches. *(above)*

### 1926: Blackburn Iris I

The first of a series of Blackburn flying boats to serve with the R.A.F., the Iris I was a long-range reconnaissance aircraft powered by three 650hp Rolls-Royce Condor engines. The first boat had a wooden hull, but subsequent versions, Mks II to V, had metal hulls and various types of engine, the Mk V acting at one time as a test bed for the Napier Gulverin diesel engine. Iris boats remained in commission until 1933. Maximum weight 32,300 lb; span 97 feet. *(top right)*

### 1926: Bristol Type 99 Badminton

In September 1925 Bristols decided to build a high-speed biplane, mainly for testing the Jupiter engine. The Type 99, Badminton, was of all-wood construction and was designed and built within seven months. The Badminton flew in the 1926 King's Cup Race but was forced to land with engine trouble. For the 1927 race the aircraft was modified with tapered wings but while practising for the race, it crashed, killing the pilot. Maximum weight (Mk I) 2,470 lb; span 24 feet. *(right)*

### 1926: Avro Avenger

Produced as a private venture, it was faster than any contemporary fighter in the R.A.F., but it failed to receive a production order. The wooden fuselage was of monocoque construction and two sets of wings were made; those illustrated, of unequal span with I-type interplane struts. The engine was a 550hp Napier Lion, and the rated maximum speed was 180 mph at sea level. The Avenger averaged 149 mph in the 1928 King's Cup race. Maximum weight (version illustrated) 3,220 lb; span 32 feet. *(left)*

### 1926: de Havilland DH66 Hercules

De Havilland's first multi-engine airliner, built to the requirements of Imperial Airways for the Cairo-Karachi section of the route to India. Powered by three Bristol Jupiter engines of 420hp, the Hercules was designed and built in less than 12 months, and served with Imperial Airways in the Middle East and in Africa until 1935. Others were sold to Australia and one survived in New Guinea until 1942. Maximum weight 15,660 lb; span 79 feet 6 inches. *(left)*

### 1926: Blackburn Ripon

Replacing the Dart as the Royal Navy's standard torpedo-reconnaissance aircraft, the prototype first flew in 1926; but the Mk II, a much-modified production version with a 570hp Napier Lion engine, did not enter service until 1929, and this was followed by the improved Mks IIA and IIC. The type was also manufactured under licence in Finland. In contrast to the Dart, the Ripon was a two-seater and it had a considerably improved performance. Maximum weight 7,400 lb; span 44 feet 10 inches. *(above)*

### 1926: Avro Avian

Built originally for the light aeroplane competition of 1926, the Avro Avian, in its various forms and with a variety of engines, was popular with owners and flying clubs between the wars. It was used for many long-distance flights, notably those by Bert Hinkler who, in 1928, flew to Australia in record time and by Kingsford Smith who again broke the record in his Avian *Southern Cross Junior* in 1930. Maximum weight (Mk IV) 1,523 lb; span 28 feet. *"Flight"* photo. *(bottom)*

### 1927: Gloster Goring

A two-seat reconnaissance bomber, built as a private venture in the hope that it might serve as a replacement for the Hawker Horsley. Fitted with a Bristol Jupiter engine of 425hp, the Goring was flown both as a landplane and as a seaplane. It had an excellent performance, being able to carry a bomb load of 695 lb with an endurance of $6\frac{1}{2}$ hours, but no production order was forthcoming. Maximum weight 5,600 lb; span 42 feet. *(below)*

### 1927: Bristol Bulldog

One of the most successful British fighters between the wars was the Bulldog. Built as a private venture, the Bulldog, fitted with a 440hp Bristol Jupiter engine, easily beat other types built to Air Ministry specification and immediately became popular with pilots. About 440 Bulldogs were built and some served with the R.A.F. until 1937. The type was also used by eight other national air forces. Maximum weight 3,350 lb; span 33 feet 10 inches. *(right)*

### 1927: Supermarine S5

For the 1927 Schneider Trophy contest, held in Venice, the R.A.F. entered a team of three aircraft, two of which were Supermarine S5s. Developed from the S4, the S5 had a low wing, wire-braced, and a still more powerful Napier Lion engine developing 875hp. The race was won by the S5 N220 with the other S5, N219, placed second; the winner's speed was 281·66 mph. Maximum weight 3,250 lb; span 26 feet 9 inches. *(below left)*

### 1927: Gloster IV

Built for the 1927 Schneider Trophy race held in Italy, the Gloster IV (nearest the camera)

represented the ultimate in racing-biplane development and was fitted with a Napier Lion engine boosted to give 875hp. In the race, which was won by a Supermarine S5, the Gloster lapped at 272·5 mph before having to retire with mechanical trouble. Three Gloster IVs were built and they were used as practice aircraft for the 1929 and 1931 races. Maximum weight 2,980 lb; span 24 feet 4 inches. *"Flight" photo. (above right)*

## 1927: Bristol Bagshot

An unusual experimental Bristol aircraft was the Bagshot twin-engine three-seat fighter designed to carry two 37-mm C.O.W. guns. The Bagshot had two 450hp Bristol Jupiter engines and the cantilever wings were of mixed steel and duralumin construction. On test the Bagshot suffered from aileron reversal due to wing flexibility under torsional loads; as a consequence development was halted and the aircraft underwent a series of static tests to investigate wing structural problems. Maximum weight 8,195 lb; span 70 feet. *(bottom)*

## 1927: Bristol Type 101

When the R.A.F.'s Fairey Foxes, with liquid-cooled engines, achieved 160 mph, the Bristol company decided to demonstrate that their new Mercury radial could provide a comparable performance. The resulting Bristol Type 101, with a 490hp Jupiter, averaged 142 mph in the 1928 King's Cup Race. Subsequently, the 101 became a Mercury testbed but in 1929 it broke up during a power dive, the pilot escaping with a parachute. Maximum weight 3,450 lb; span 33 feet 7 inches. *(centre left)*

## 1928: Vickers Vildebeest

Built as a replacement for the Hawker Horsley, the Vildebeest torpedo bomber entered service with the R.A.F. in 1932, and some were still operational when the Japanese invaded in 1941. The Vildebeest also served with the R.N.Z.A.F. and 26 were built in Spain. Most of the Vildebeests were Mk IIIs with 635hp Bristol Pegasus engines. A general purpose and army cooperation variant known as the Vincent also served with the R.A.F. Maximum weight (Mk III) 8,500 lb; span 49 feet. *(below)*

## 1928: Supermarine Solent

Built originally as a torpedo-carrying aircraft for the Danish Navy, the Solent was similar to the Southampton but with a modified wing structure and powered by three Armstrong Siddeley Jaguar engines of 420hp. The aircraft was not delivered to Denmark and was civilianised in September 1928 as a private aircraft for the Hon. A. E. Guinness, and used for journeys between Southampton and the Irish ports until it was scrapped in 1934. Maximum weight 16,300 lb; span 75 feet. *(above)*

### 1928: Hawker Tomtit

The Tomtit was built as a replacement for the Avro 504N, but was produced in only limited quantities for both R.A.F. and civilian use; others were exported to Canada and New Zealand. The standard Tomtit had an Armstrong Siddeley Mongoose engine with the Cirrus Hermes offered as an alternative. One Tomtit was used as a flying test-bed for the Wolseley radial engine. Maximum weight 1,750 lb; span 28 feet 7 inches. *(above)*

### 1928: Hawker Hart

The Hart set new standards in the R.A.F. and, between the wars, more Harts and Hart variants were built than any other type of aircraft in Great Britain. With its Rolls-Royce Kestrel engine the Hart day bomber easily outpaced the R.A.F.'s fighters, and versions for training, army cooperation, fighting and deck-landing were built in quantity. Harts and Hart variants were exported to at least 16 countries. Maximum weight 4,500 lb; span 37 feet 3 inches. *(top right)*

### 1929: Vickers Type 143 "Bolivian Scout"

A fighter which saw active service in the Gran Chaco war between Bolivia and Paraguay (1932-35) was the Type 143 powered by a 450hp Bristol Jupiter engine, six of which were supplied to the Bolivian Air Force. The Type 143, known henceforth as the "Bolivian Scout", had a maximum speed of 150 mph and was one of a series of single-engine monoplane and biplane fighters built by Vickers which culminated in the Venom. Maximum weight 3,120 lb; span 34 feet. *(above left)*

### 1929: Supermarine Seamew

Following the success of the Southampton, Supermarines produced a smaller version, the Seamew, an amphibian flying boat built to Air Ministry specification 31/24 and powered by two 240hp Armstrong Siddeley Lynx engines. Two aircraft were completed but there was no production order. An unusual feature was the crew arrangement with the pilot situated in the extreme nose with a raised gunner's position immediately aft. Another

gunner's station was positioned
behind the wings. Maximum
weight 6,500 lb; span 46 feet.
*(opposite page centre)*

### 1929: Supermarine S6

For the 1929 Schneider Trophy
contest Supermarine produced a
new design, the S6, to take a
special racing engine developed
by Rolls-Royce. Based on the
850hp Buzzard V 12-cylinder
engine, the new "R" engine had
a larger supercharger and other
refinements and developed
1,900hp. The S6, N247, won the
contest at a speed of
328·63 mph. After the event the
S6 set a new world's speed
record of 357·7 mph. Maximum
weight 5,771 lb; span 30 feet.
*(opposite page bottom)*

### 1929: Gloster VI

The Gloster company's last
Schneider Trophy aircraft was
the Gloster VI, two of which
were built for the 1929 contest.
For this race the Napier Lion
engine had again been uprated to
give more than 1,300hp, but it
proved unreliable and the
Gloster monoplanes had to be
withdrawn from the race. Three
days later, the engine having
been persuaded to run for long

enough, one of the Glosters
succeeded in breaking the
world's speed record at
336·3 mph. Span 26 feet. *(left)*

### 1929: Avro Tutor

Following the tradition of the
famous 504 series and serving as
a replacement of the 504N, the
Tutor became the standard
trainer of the R.A.F. and it was
also used by some 14 overseas
air forces. The Tutor, powered
by an Armstrong Siddeley Lynx
engine of 240hp, remained with
the R.A.F. until it was finally
replaced in 1938, but several
civilian Tutors survived the war
and one is now preserved in
flying condition. Maximum
weight 2,500 lb; span 34 feet.
*"Flight" photo. (bottom)*

### 1929: de Havilland DH80 Puss Moth

The growth of air touring in the late 1920s led to the production of the DH 80 Puss Moth with an inverted four-cylinder Gipsy III engine of 120hp. The Puss Moth was used for many long-distance flights, including Mollison's solo east-to-west crossing of the North Atlantic in *The Heart's Content,* illustrated above, in 1932. In 1933 the Puss Moth was superseded by the similar Leopard Moth with a better performance. Maximum weight 2,100 lb; span 30 feet 11 inches. *(above right)*

### 1929: Supermarine Air Yacht

This three-engine, monoplane flying boat, ordered by the Hon. A. E. Guinness was unusual in having stabilising sponsons in place of the more usual wing-tip floats. The Air Yacht was of all-metal construction and had accommodation for a crew of three and six passengers with 600 lb of baggage. The original 490hp Armstrong Siddeley Jaguar engines were later replaced by Armstrong Siddeley Panthers. Maximum weight 25,000 lb; span 92 feet. *(top right)*

### 1929: Vickers Type 150

In an effort to provide a night-bomber replacement for the long-serving Virginia, Vickers submitted a twin-engine biplane the Type 150, to meet specification B19/27. Originally powered by Rolls-Royce FX IV engines, which had evaporative cooling that proved to be unsatisfactory, a change was made to two Bristol Pegasus engines. The aircraft was also extensively modified in several important respects, including the replacement of the single-bay wings with a two-bay structure. Maximum weight 16,103 lb; span 27 feet 6 inches. *(opposite page top right)*

### 1930 Vickers Viastra

Basically, a 10 to 12 passenger, high-wing metal monoplane, employing the patent Wibault type of construction. Eight Viastra variants were built featuring one, two and three engine layouts. Two Viastra IIs, with two 525hp Bristol Jupiter engines, served with varying success in Australia, while another, a Mk X, with two Bristol Pegasus engines, was supplied for the use of the

Prince of Wales—later King Edward VIII. Maximum weight (Mk II) 12,350 lb; span 70 feet. *(above centre)*

### 1930: Blackburn Sydney

Built as a possible successor to the Iris, this was Great Britain's first large monoplane flying-boat. It was powered by three 525hp Rolls-Royce FX11 engines and had a top speed of more than 120 mph. The Sydney did not go into production and only one was built. It was used for research flying at the Marine Aircraft Experimental Establishment's base at Felixstowe until it was dismantled in 1934. Maximum weight 20,700 lb; span 100 feet. *(left)*

### 1930: Armstrong Whitworth AW16

Designed primarily as a Fleet fighter, this aircraft was also intended to be suitable for day-and-night fighter duties. It was powered by an Armstrong Siddeley Panther engine developing 525hp. The AW16 was in competition with Gloster and Hawker aircraft, but the order went elsewhere. Subsequently the AW16 was used as a test bed for the Armstrong Siddeley Hyena, an experimental engine that was eventually abandoned. Maximum speed 195 mph at 15,000 feet. Maximum weight 3,600 lb; span 33 feet. *"Flight" photo. (above)*

### 1931: Vickers Type 163

Fitted with four Rolls-Royce Kestrel engines, this aircraft was originally conceived as a troop carrier and heavy night-bomber. Subsequently it was considered as a battleplane carrying a 37 mm C.O.W. gun and three other machine-gun positions; in addition, it was also intended to perform its original duties as a heavy night bomber and troop carrier. As eventually built, the 163 had a crew of five and accommodation for 21 troops. Produced as a private venture, the 163 was not ordered into production. Maximum weight 25,700 lb; span 90 feet. *(above left)*

**1931: Hawker Fury**
With a 525hp Rolls-Royce
Kestrel engine, the Fury, like the
Hart, was built in large numbers
for the R.A.F. and some seven
overseas air forces. It was the
first of the R.A.F.'s fighters to
exceed 200 mph; a deck-flying
version called the Nimrod served
with the Royal Navy. The Fury
remained in service with the
R.A.F. until 1939, when it
finally gave place to the
Hurricane. Maximum weight
3,600 lb; span 30 feet. *(right)*

### 1931: Blackburn B2 Trainer

Considered as a lineal descendant of the Bluebird, this aircraft retained the side-by-side seating arrangement of its forerunner. The B2 was of all-metal construction except for the wing covering, and was fitted with various types of de Havilland and Blackburn engines. Maximum weight 1,770 lb; span 30 feet 2 inches. *(right)*

### 1931: Supermarine S6B

The 1931 Schneider Trophy was won in a "fly-over" by an S6B at a speed of 340·8 mph. The S6B was a modified and slightly larger version of the S6, winner of the 1929 contest. The Rolls-Royce "R" engine of the S6B had been further developed to deliver 2,300 bhp. Subsequently the S6B twice raised the world's speed record, first to 379·05 mph and then, with a boosted engine, to 407·5 mph. Maximum weight 6,086 lb; span 30 feet. *(left centre)*

### 1931: de Havilland Tiger Moth

This aircraft, and the Avro 504 together rank among the most famous training machines ever produced. Developed well before the second war, and exported to many countries, the Tiger Moth, with its inverted Gipsy Major engine, was a direct descendant of the DH60 Moth. As the R.A.F.'s standard elementary trainer, the Tiger Moth was built in thousands at home and in Australia, Canada, and New Zealand. Maximum weight 1,825 lb; span 29 feet 4 inches. *"Flight" photo. (left bottom)*

### 1932: Supermarine Scapa

A much modified and cleaned-up version of the Southampton, which was originally known as the Southampton Mk IV; a general reconnaissance flying boat, with a crew of five. The aircraft had an all-metal structure and the engines were two Rolls-Royce Kestrels, each of 525hp, giving the Scapa a top speed of more than 140 mph; 15 Scapas were built, and the type served with the R.A.F. from 1934 until 1938. Maximum weight of 16,040 lb; span 75 feet. *(right)*

### 1932: Airspeed AS4 Ferry

The first product of the Airspeed Company had been a glider, but the next aircraft to emerge was the AS4 Ferry, designed specially for joy-riding from small fields with National Aviation Day Displays. Powered by three de Havilland Gipsy engines, two upright and one inverted, it carried ten passengers. Only four Ferries were built, but two of them were used on internal services between the North of England, Scotland, and Ulster. Maximum weight 5,400 lb; span 55 feet. *"Flight" photo. (below left)*

### 1932: Armstrong Whitworth Atalanta

This aircraft represented a considerable step forward in British airliner design; it was tailored specially for operation on the African route of Imperial Airways and had four Armstrong Siddeley Serval engines of 340hp, and seats for 17 passengers. Eight Atalantas were built and they served the African and Indian routes until 1939. After the outbreak of war they were used as coastal patrol aircraft by the Indian Air Force. Maximum weight 21,000 lb; span 90 feet. *"Flight" photo. (below)*

### 1932: Blackburn Baffin

This replacement for the Ripon was to become the standard torpedo-bomber of the Fleet Air Arm, first entering service in 1934 and embarking on its career in the carrier *H.M.S. Glorious.* Similar in most respects to the Ripon, the Baffin had a more powerful Bristol Pegasus air-cooled radial engine developing 580 bhp. Baffins also served with the Royal New Zealand Air Force and were used operationally in the Pacific area until 1941. Maximum weight 7,700 lb; span 45 feet 6 inches. *(left)*

### 1932: de Havilland DH84 Dragon

An economical light aircraft, evolved to meet the requirements of a motor-coach operator who believed he could operate a cut-price air service to Paris. The Dragon, which carried six passengers and 114 mph with two 130hp Gipsy Major engines, did, in fact, make this possible. The Dragon also found a ready market at home and overseas, and it was built in large numbers in England and Australia. Maximum weight 4,500 lb; span 47 feet 4 inches. *(left)*

### 1932: Gloster Gauntlet

One of the outstanding fighters of the '30s, which entered service with the R.A.F. in 1935. Powered by a Bristol Mercury engine, the Gauntlet was itself the production version of the Gloster SS18 and SS19. The Gauntlet was the fastest fighter in the R.A.F. until 1937, and it was the subject of special tests to determine the reason for its exceptionally low drag. Some Gauntlets served with the R.A.F. until 1939. Maximum weight 3,950 lb; span 32 feet 10 inches. *(bottom)*

### 1933: Supermarine Walrus Amphibian

The prototype of this aircraft was first ordered by the Australian government. Later, in 1935, the Walrus was put into production for the R.A.F. and the Royal Navy, and the type was still in front-line service at the end of the 1939-'45 war. Powered by a 775hp Bristol Pegasus engine, the Walrus was carried on the catapults of battleships and cruisers of the Royal Navy. A total of 741 was built. Maximum weight 7,200 lb; span 45 feet 10 inches. *Imperial War Museum photo. (above right)*

forced the aircraft down in Malta. Another Courier came third in the handicap section of the 1934 London-to-Melbourne race. Maximum weight 3,900 lb; span 47 feet. *(below)*

### 1933: Blackburn Shark

Built in greater numbers than any previous Blackburn aircraft, the Shark served with the Royal Navy from 1935 until the late war years, by which time it had been relegated to target-towing and instructional duties. The Shark was used by the Portuguese Navy and was also built in Canada. The seaplane version illustrated below formed part of the equipment of several British battle cruisers in the years between the wars. Maximum weight (seaplane) 8,745 lb; span 45 feet. *(bottom)*

### 1933: Blackburn Perth

A larger and more powerful version of the Iris flying boat, the Perth was notable for the fact that it mounted a 37 mm "anti-shipping" cannon, capable of firing $1\frac{1}{2}$ lb shells at the rate of 10 a minute. The Perth carried a crew of five, and formed the equipment of No. 209 Squadron R.A.F., based on Plymouth. With its three 825hp Rolls-Royce Buzzard engines, it had a top speed of 132 mph. Maximum weight 32,500 lb; span 97 feet. *(above)*

### 1933: Airspeed AS5 Courier

The first aircraft in Great Britain to go into production with a retractable undercarriage—generally considered at the time to be more trouble than it was worth. The first Courier was used for an attempted non-stop flight to India with air refuelling en route, but mechanical trouble

## 1934: de Havilland DH89 Dragon Rapide

An improved version of the Dragon, this aircraft proved to be one of the most successful light transport aeroplanes of the era and it achieved world-wide sales. With seats for up to eight passengers and powered by two 200hp Gipsy Six engines, the Rapide has been widely used for airline and charter work and, as the Dominie, it served during the war as a transport and as a trainer. Maximum weight 5,500 lb; span 48 feet. *(above)*

## 1934: de Havilland DH86 Airliner

This aircraft was designed to a QANTAS specification for operation on the Singapore-Darwin section of the England-Australia route. The type was also used by Imperial Airways, Railway Air Services, Jersey Airways and many other airlines. During the war it served throughout as a transport with the Royal Navy and with the R.A.F. With four 200hp de Havilland Gipsy Six engines, the DH86 could carry up to 12 passengers. Maximum weight 10,250 lb; span 64 feet 6 inches. *(right)*

## 1934: Armstrong Whitworth AW35 Scimitar

A much-modified version of the AW16, this aircraft was the last pre-war fighter designed by the Company and represented the ultimate development of the air-cooled-engine-biplane formula. The prototype aircraft was powered by an Armstrong Siddeley Panther engine of 600hp, but the four aircraft delivered to Norway had a more powerful version developing 730hp. No orders were received at home and only six aircraft were built. Maximum weight 4,100 lb; span 33 feet. *(right)*

## 1934: de Havilland DH88 Comet

Prizes worth £15,000 put up for the London-Melbourne race in 1934 attracted entries from many nations, including the USA, and the de Havilland company set about building a special aircraft

for the event—the DH88 Comet.
This was the first British aircraft
to incorporate together a
retractable undercarriage, wing
flaps, and two-position
propellers. The winning Comet
flew from London to Melbourne
(with six intermediate stops) in
70 hours 54 minutes. Maximum
weight 5,550 lb; span 44 feet.
*(above)*

## 1934: Mew Gull

This name covered five Percival
racing monoplanes which
differed in detail but which
achieved numerous successes in
racing and record-breaking. The
first, G-ACND, with a 165hp
Napier Javelin engine, lapped at
191 mph in the 1934 King's Cup
before being rebuilt with a
200hp de Havilland Gipsy Six

engine. The fastest, G-AFAA,
also with a Gipsy Six engine,
had a reduced span and achieved
a maximum speed exceeding
235 mph. Maximum weight
2,125 lb; span 22 feet 9 inches.
*"Flight" photo. (top)*

**1934: Gloster Gladiator**
Last of the R.A.F.'s biplane fighters, the Gladiator was still in front-line service at the outbreak of the 1939-'45 war. The Royal Navy's Sea Gladiators saw service in Norway, the Mediterranean, and the North Sea before being withdrawn in 1941. This type is also famous for its part played (by three aircraft) in the defence of Malta in 1940. The Gladiator had an 830hp Bristol Mercury engine and, unusual in a biplane, split trailing-edge flaps. Production aircraft differed from the prototype illustrated by having an enclosed cockpit. Maximum weight 4,650 lb; span 32 feet 3 inches. *(below)*

### 1935: Supermarine Stranraer

Originally known as the Southampton Mk V, this aircraft was ordered to specification 17/35. Production Stranraers were powered by two 875hp Bristol Pegasus engines and of all-metal structure with fabric-covered wings. The Stranraer entered service with the R.A.F. in 1936 and served with three squadrons of Coastal Command until superseded by Sunderlands and Lerwicks in 1940. The Stranraer was also built in Canada and served with the R.C.A.F. Maximum weight 19,000 lb; span 85 feet. *"Flight" photo. (opposite page top)*

### 1935: Bristol Type 42

*Britain First,* a Type 142 transport monoplane, was a private venture design one of which was ordered by Lord Rothermere, the Press baron, as a boost for British aviation. With two 650hp Bristol Mercury engines, four passengers and a crew of two, *Britain First* achieved 307 mph, some 50 mph faster than current R.A.F. fighters. Lord Rothermere presented the aircraft to the nation and from it was developed the Bristol Blenheim. Maximum weight 9,357 lb; span 56 feet 4 inches. *(above)*

### 1935: Avro Anson

This famous aircraft started life as a small airliner, the Avro 652, with Imperial Airways but was later modified for coastal patrol duties. The first monoplane to join the R.A.F., the Anson operated with Coastal Command until 1942 after which it was used for training and communication. The last Anson, pictured above, was delivered in 1952 after 11,000 had been built. The Anson had two Armstrong Siddeley Cheetah engines. Maximum weight 9,450 lb; span 56 feet 6 inches. *(top)*

### 1935: Vickers Wellesley

Vickers' private venture contestant for Air Ministry specification G.4/31 was the Wellesley, employing fully, and for the first time, the Geodetic form of construction evolved by Sir Barnes Wallis. This resulted in a clean cantilever monoplane with a very low structure weight. Power was supplied by a 925hp Bristol Pegasus engine. Altogether, 176 Wellesleys were delivered to the R.A.F. and they saw action in the Middle East and East African theatres. Maximum weight 11,000 lb; span 74 feet 7 inches. *(top)*

### 1935: Percival Vega Gull

Developed from the Gull Six, the Vega Gull was one of the most popular touring aircraft of its time. With a 200hp de Havilland Gipsy Six engine, the Vega Gull carried four people and cruised at 150 mph. It was much used for racing, winning both the King's Cup race and the Portsmouth-Johannesburg race in 1936. A total of 89 Vega Gulls was built before the war halted production. Maximum weight 3,250 lb; span 39 feet 6 inches. *"Flight" photo. (above)*

### 1935: Hawker Hurricane

The first order for 600 examples of this immortal fighter was placed in 1936, soon after the prototype's first flight; but because of the introduction of the new mark of Rolls-Royce Merlin, production was delayed until 1937. However by the end of 1938 some 200 aircraft had been delivered and, by the time the Battle of Britain started, the R.A.F. possessed 26 Hurricane squadrons. The Hurricane served throughout the war, and more than 14,500 were built. Maximum weight (Mk IV) 8,450 lb; span 40 feet. *(right)*

### 1935: Bristol Bombay

This troop transport was designed to a specification drawn up in 1931. It was powered by two 1,010hp Bristol Pegasus engines and had accommodation for 24 troops. The Bombay was ordered into production in 1937 and, because Bristol's Filton factory was then busy building Blenheims, the 50 Bombays ordered were built by Short and Harland. After supplying troops in France in 1940, most of the Bombays were transferred to the Middle East. Maximum weight 20,000 lb; span 95 feet 9 inches. *(below)*

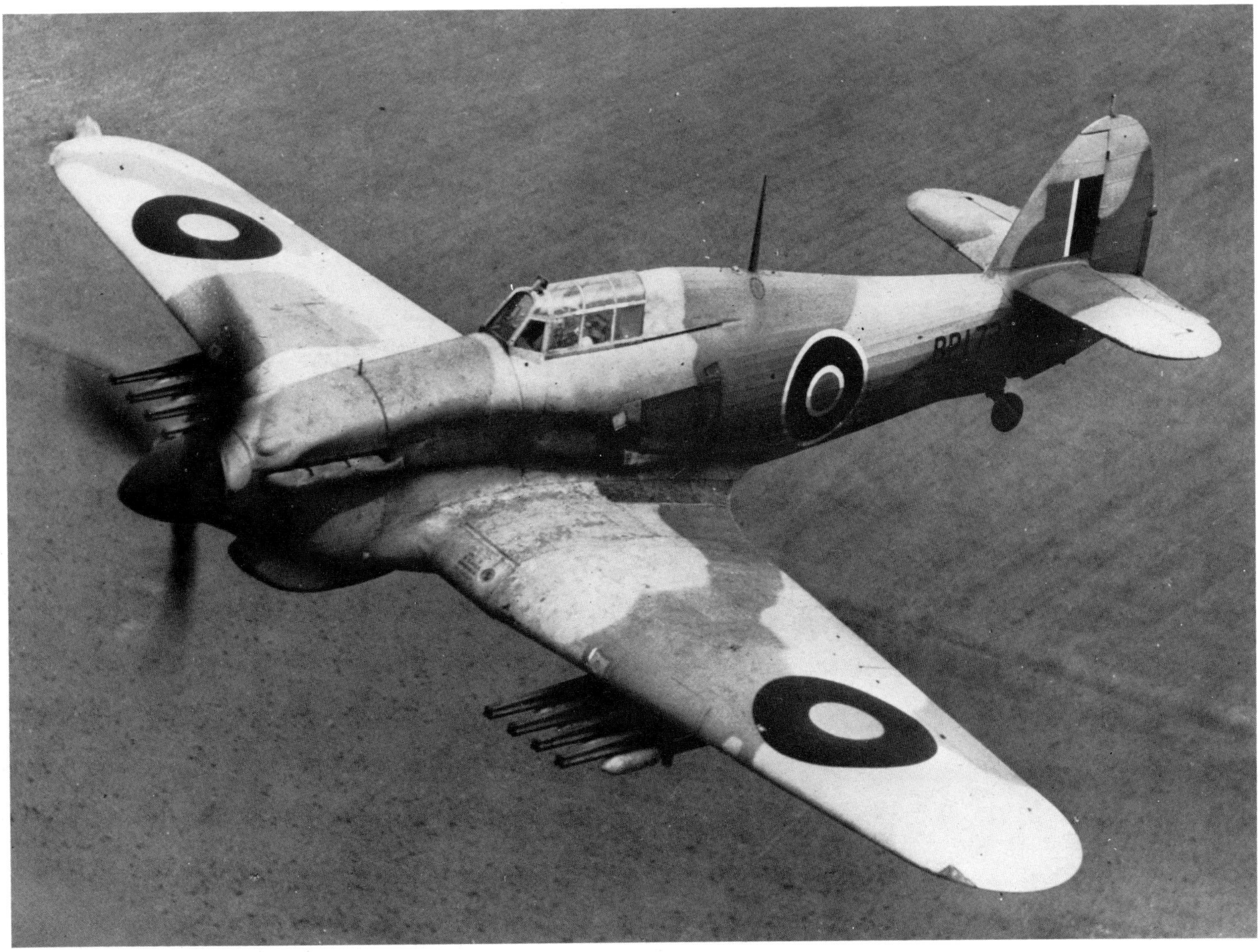

**1936: Vickers Venom**
Powered by a 625hp Bristol
Aquila engine, this aircraft was
an attempt to provide an
advanced fighter using an air-
cooled, radial engine. The
aircraft, armed with eight guns,
had a speed of 312 mph, was
more manoeuvrable and had a
higher rate of roll than the more
powerful Merlin-engined fighters
which were chosen for
production, but the Venom
served to disprove the myth that
a radial-engined fighter had no
future. Maximum weight
4,156 lb; span 32 feet 9 inches.
*(below)*

**1936: Bristol Type 138A**
Designed to capture the altitude
record and powered by a 500hp
Bristol Pegasus engine, the Type
138A was a large, single-seat
monoplane with an enclosed but
unpressurised cockpit, the pilot
being protected by a pressurised
suit and breathing apparatus.
The Bristol 138A twice broke the
record: on September 28, 1936,
it reached 49,967 feet, breaking
the existing French record.
Subsequently, on June 30 1937,
it reached 53,937 feet, breaking
an Italian record. Maximum
weight 5,310 lb; span 66 feet.
*(bottom)*

### 1936: Supermarine Spitfire

The only Allied fighter to remain in continuous production throughout the 1939-'45 war. Altogether, 18 marks were produced, and the speed rose from 355 to 454 mph. Spitfires were first ordered in June 1936 and, by 1940, there were 19 R.A.F. Spitfire squadrons ready for the Battle of Britain. Production eventually reached 20,351. Most Spitfires had Rolls-Royce Merlin engines, but later versions had the Rolls-Royce Griffon. Maximum weight (Mk V) 6,417 lb; span 36 feet 10 inches. *Ministry of Defence photo. (left)*

### 1936: Armstrong Whitworth Whitley

One of the three bomber types that formed the equipment of Bomber Command at the beginning of the war. It is remembered for the early leaflet raids and for having dropped the first bombs on German soil in March 1940. It was also used extensively by Coastal Command and later as tug at glider training schools. Early Whitleys were fitted with two Armstrong Siddeley Tiger engines, but later marks had Rolls-Royce Merlins. Maximum weight (Mk V) 28,200 lb; span 84 feet. *(below)*

**1936: Bristol Blenheim**
Derived directly from the Bristol
Type 142, *Britain First,* the
Blenheim Type 142M was
designed as a medium bomber.
It differed from its predecessor
in having a midwing layout, a
dorsal gun turret, and more
powerful Bristol Mercury engines
of 920hp. The Blenheim was
ordered into production in
December 1936 and it joined the
R.A.F. in March 1937. More
than 6,200 of the many
Blenheim variants were built,
and it had a distinguished war
record. Maximum weight
(Blenheim IV) 12,500 lb; span
56 feet 4 inches. *(below)*

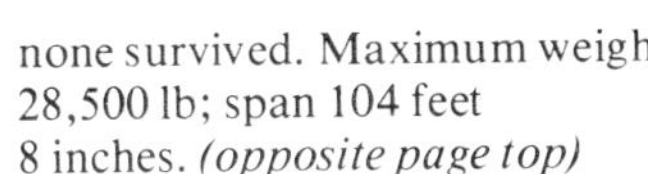

### 1937: Blackburn Skua

This was the first monoplane to become standard equipment with the Fleet Air Arm. It was also the Navy's first dive-bomber. Powered by a Bristol Perseus engine, it entered service in 1938 and it has the distinction of being the first British aircraft to destroy an enemy aeroplane during the war. Later, in April 1940, Skuas dive-bombed and sank the German cruiser *Konigsberg* in Bergen harbour. Maximum weight 8,230 lb; span 40 feet 2 inches. *(left)*

### 1937: Airspeed Oxford

Widely used as an advanced trainer before and during the war, not only in Britain but in Canada, Rhodesia, Australia and New Zealand. The standard engine was the Armstrong Siddeley 370 hp Cheetah, but some Oxfords had 450 hp Pratt and Whitney radials. The Oxford was developed from the similar civil Envoy and after the war it was modified again for civil use and known as the Consul. Maximum weight 8,000 lb; span 53 feet 4 inches. *"Flight" photo. (below)*

### 1937: de Havilland DH91 Albatross

One of the cleanest piston-engined airliners ever built, the DH91 was designed as a trans-Atlantic mail plane to carry a payload of 1,000 lb for 2,500 miles against headwinds of 40 mph. Built on the plywood-and-balsa sandwich principle, the Albatross had four de Havilland Gipsy Twelve engines, each of 525hp. Albatrosses served as transports with B.O.A.C. during the war, but none survived. Maximum weight 28,500 lb; span 104 feet 8 inches. *(opposite page top)*

### 1937: Airspeed Queen Wasp

This pilotless, radio-controlled aircraft was designed to provide a faster and more realistic gunnery target than the Queen Bee. The Queen Wasp was flown originally as a landplane with a pilot, but operationally it was a seaplane capable, even in 1937, of making fully automatic landings. By the time the Queen Wasp was ready for production, in 1940, the need for it had passed; there were other targets to shoot at. Maximum weight 3,500 lb; span 31 feet. *Imperial War Museum photo. (centre left)*

### 1937: Percival Q6 Petrel

This light transport aircraft was Percival's first with twin engines. The standard Q6 had a fixed undercarriage, but a retractable version was available. The Q6 was powered by de Havilland Gipsy Six engines of 200 hp, which gave the fixed-undercarriage aircraft a cruising speed of some 170 mph. Production, cut short by the war, totalled 15 aircraft, of which at least 10 served with the R.A.F. Maximum weight 5,500 lb; span 46 feet 8 inches. *"Flight" photo. (bottom left)*

### 1936: Vickers Wellington

This aircraft benefitted in full from the Geodetic form of construction, and it proved to be one of the outstanding aircraft of its time. Wellingtons formed the backbone of the R.A.F.'s Bomber Command during the early phase of the war, and they were also used by Coastal and Transport Commands as well as a variety of other duties. The total number of Wellingtons built reached 11,640, the largest number of a single British bomber type ever built. Maximum weight 31,000 lb; span 86 feet 2 inches. *(bottom right)*

### 1938: de Havilland DH95 Flamingo

This aircraft showed every promise of world-wide sales until the war cut short its career. With two 890 hp Bristol Perseus engines, and accommodation for up to 17 passengers, the Flamingo was the first all-metal, stressed-skin aircraft to be built by de Havilland. During the war Flamingoes served with the R.A.F., and the Royal Navy, and with B.O.A.C. in the Middle East. One survived the war and operated on charter work until 1949. Maximum weight 18,000 lb; span 70 feet. *(below)*

### 1938: Supermarine Sea Otter

Designed as a replacement for the Walrus, this aircraft had an 855 hp Bristol Mercury engine driving a tractor airscrew, which gave the aircraft a greater range with a bigger load, and an improved take-off as compared with its predecessor. The Sea Otter was the last Supermarine amphibian to go into production and it did particularly valuable work in the air-sea rescue role in home waters and in the Far East. Total production amounted to 290. Maximum weight 10,000 lb; span 46 feet. *Imperial War Museum photo.* *(bottom)*

### 1938: Bristol Beaufort

Designed as a torpedo-bomber to replace the Vickers Vildebeest, and first ordered in 1936, the Beaufort was powered by two 1,130 hp Bristol Taurus engines, though some had Pratt and Whitney Twin Wasps of 1,200 hp. Beauforts saw much action in home waters, in the Atlantic and the Mediterranean, as well as against the Japanese with the R.A.A.F. Altogether, 2,129 Beauforts were produced, including 700 built in Australia. Maximum weight 22,500 lb; span 57 feet 10 inches. *(right)*

**1938: Armstrong Whitworth Ensign**

An ambitious 40-passenger airliner for Imperial Airways, though preoccupation with the Whitley and the many alterations demanded by the customer delayed production. Originally powered by four 850 hp Armstrong Siddeley Tiger engines, the Ensign was underpowered and was re-engined with Wright Cyclones of 950 hp. After the declaration of war Ensigns were employed as war transports, on which duty two were captured and five destroyed. Maximum weight 54,000 lb; span 123 feet. *(above left)*

# 1939: THE SECOND WORLD WAR

### 1939: Vickers Warwick

Designed as a bomber, this was an enlarged version of the Wellington. Initially, it suffered from the underdevelopment of its intended engines; later it was fitted with Pratt and Whitney Double Wasp, or 2,500hp Bristol Centaurus engines. By then, the four-engine bombers were entering service and the Warwicks were used as freighters or dropping parachute-launched motor life-boats for air-sea rescue. Maximum weight (ASR Mk 1) 45,000 lb; span 96 feet 9 inches. *Imperial War Museum photo. (above centre)*

### 1939: Percival Proctor

A development of the Vega Gull, the Proctor 3-seat communication aircraft, powered by a 210hp de Havilland Gipsy Queen engine, was built in large numbers and used for many duties including radio and navigational training for both the Royal Navy and the R.A.F. The final R.A.F. version was the Proctor 4, redesigned as a 4-seater, while the Proctor 5 was a post-war civil variant. Maximum weight (Proctor 4) 3,500 lb; span 39 feet 6 inches. *Imperial War Museum photo. (above)*

### 1939: Bristol Beaufighter

With two Pegasus engines, a crew of two, four 20-mm cannons, and an early version of the airborne interceptor radar, the Beaufighter joined the R.A.F. in 1940; during 1941 the number of night raiders destroyed rose from three in January to 96 in May. Later, armed with bombs, rockets or torpedoes, the Beaufighter was equally successful against enemy shipping. Maximum weight 25,400 lb; span 57 feet 10 inches. *(above)*

### 1939: Avro Manchester

This bomber was powered by two Rolls-Royce 1,760hp Vulture engines, each with 24 cylinder arranged in the form of an X. The Manchester entered service with Bomber Command in 1940 and took part in the famous "Thousand Bomber Raid" on Cologne in 1941. However, the Vulture engine was insufficiently developed and proved a failure, making it necessary to withdraw the Manchester from operations in the summer of 1942. Maximum weight 56,000 lb; span 90 feet 1 inch. *(right centre)*

### 1940: Hawker Typhoon

This proved to be one of the most formidable fighters of the war. In its early days is suffered from teething troubles, as did its unconventional Napier Sabre engine, but with the arrival of the Mk II, the Typhoon began to show its worth. It was the fastest Allied fighter low-down, and it excelled at ground-strafing, in which role it was much in evidence, after the D-Day landings. maximum weight 13,250 lb; span 41 feet 7 inches. *(above right)*

### 1940: Armstrong Whitworth Albemarle

A reconnaissance bomber with two 1,590hp Bristol Hercules engines, built of steel and wood as an insurance against a possible shortage of light alloy. It was made up of sub-assemblies made almost entirely by sub-contractors. Production was delayed and the Albemarle was never used as a bomber, but it served as a glider tug, taking part in the invasion of Normandy and in the assault on Arnhem. Maximum weight 22,600 lb; span 77 feet. *(far right)*

### 1940: de Havilland DH98 Mosquito

Developed in spite of considerable official opposition and one of the most versatile aircraft of the war. Built of wood and with two Rolls-Royce Merlin engines, it was among the fastest aircraft until early 1944. Among its many duties were bombing, day-and-night fighting, photo-reconnaissance, ground strafing, torpedo-carrying and deck-landing and the carriage of passengers and freight. The Mosquito continued to serve with the R.A.F. until 1955. Maximum weight 23,850 lb; span 54 feet 2 inches. *(right)*

### 1941: Avro Lancaster

Following the failure of the Manchester's Vulture engines, drastic steps were taken to modify the airframe to take four Rolls-Royce Merlins; thus was born the Avro Lancaster, the most successful of all the wartime heavy bombers. Among the many notable actions in which the Lancaster took part were the bombing of the Mohne Dam and the devastating attack on the rocket base at Peenemunde in 1943. Altogether, 7,377 Lancasters were built. Maximum weight 70,000 lb; span 103 feet. *(below)*

### 1941: Gloster E28/39 Pioneer

Sometimes described as the biggest step forward since the Wright Brothers' first aeroplane, the jet engine was first flown in England in an aircraft built by Glosters. It was fitted with the Whittle W1 engine which initially gave about 860 lb of thrust. The historic first flight took place on May 15, 1941 and development continued rapidly. In April 1943 the E28/39, by now known as the Pioneer, was demonstrated to Winston Churchill at Hatfield. Maximum weight 3,750 lb; span 29 feet. *(right)*

### 1941: Airspeed Horsa

Designed and built by the Airspeed company within the space of ten months. Main production, apart from those built at Airspeed's Christchurch factory, was by woodworking firms and furniture manufacturers who made up sub-assemblies for erection at R.A.F. maintenance units. The glider carried two pilots and 25

troops, and it was used in the invasions of Sicily and Normandy and later at Arnhem and at the Rhine crossing. Maximum weight 15,500 lb; span 88 feet. *Imperial War Museum photo. (right)*

## 1942: Hawker Tempest

The last Hawker aircraft to see active service during the second war, and a development of the Typhoon with a thinner wing to improve the high-speed characteristics. The first version had a Napier Sabre engine. but later marks were powered by the Bristol Centaurus developing 2,520hp. With this engine the Tempest II, illustrated above, had a top speed of 442 mph and it proved an effective weapon against the flying bomb. Maximum weight 13,250 lb; span 41 feet. *(top right)*

## 1942: Blackburn Firebrand

This aircraft suffered more than most from the vacillations of official policy; starting in 1942 as a single-seat fighter with a Napier Sabre engine, it was re-designed as a single-seat torpedo carrier. This version was followed by the Mk 3 with a Bristol Centaurus engine, and the Mk 4 which finally went into production. The Mk 4, illustrated, and the Mk 5 which followed, served until 1953. Maximum weight (Mk 4) 15,670 lb; span 51 feet 3 inches. *(right)*

## 1942: Avro York

The success of the Lancaster led to the production of the Avro York, a transport version, with a commodious fuselage but with Lancaster wings, engines, undercarriage and tail surfaces. Because Great Britain had agreed with America to concentrate on military aircraft, York production commenced only in 1945. By 1948 the R.A.F. had six squadrons and the York was also used by BOAC, BSAA and other airlines, and it continued in commercial use until the 1960s. Maximum weight 68,000 lb; span 102 feet. *(right)*

## 1943: de Havilland DH100 Vampire

The first de Havilland jet aircraft, powered by a de Havilland Goblin engine initially developing 3,000 lb of thrust. The Vampire just missed the war, but it served in the peacetime R.A.F. as a fighter, nightfighter and as a trainer; it was also used by more than a dozen overseas air forces. A Vampire with a Ghost engine broke the world's altitude record in 1948, reaching 59,446 feet. Maximum weight 12,360 lb; span 38 feet. *(above)*

## 1943: Vickers Windsor

This heavy bomber arrived too late for active service and production orders were cancelled in 1945. The Windsor was unusual in having a single-wheel retractable undercarriage under each of its four 1,635hp Rolls-Royce Merlin engines. Construction was based on the Geodetic principle with fabric covering. An experimental feature of one of the three prototypes was a pair of remotely-controlled gun barbettes behind the inboard engines. Maximum weight 54,000 lb; span 117 feet 2 inches. *(opposite page, centre left)*

## 1943: Gloster Meteor

The first jet aircraft to enter service with the R.A.F. and the only Allied jet to see action during the second war. The first production aircraft had two Rolls-Royce Welland engines, and was used with success against the flying bombs. The Meteor twice broke the World's speed record, the second time at 616 mph. Altogether some seven main marks were developed and total production exceeded 3,300 aircraft. Maximum weight (Mk 8) 15,675 lb; span 37 feet 2 inches. *(opposite page top)*

## 1944: Supermarine Spiteful

Intended as a replacement for the Spitfire, the Spiteful was just

entering service when the war ended. Only about 17 were completed and production was cancelled in May 1945. The final version, the Spiteful F16, with a 2,420hp Rolls-Royce Griffon engine, achieved a speed of 494 mph. Production of a Naval version, the Seafang, was also cancelled at the end of the war. Maximum weight (Spiteful) 10,200 lb; span 35 feet 6 inches. *"Flight" photo. (above)*

## 1944: Avro Lincoln

Designed to replace the Lancaster, the Lincoln was introduced just too late for the war, but it remained the mainstay of Bomber Command until the end of 1955, and was the last of the R.A.F.'s piston-engined bombers. The Lincoln had four 1,750hp Rolls-Royce Merlin engines and fuel for 3,500 miles. It was used as a test bed for numerous turbine engines, including the Derwent, Avon and the Tyne. Maximum weight 82,000 lb; span 120 feet. *(left)*

## 1944: de Havilland DH Hornet

With two 2,070hp Rolls-Royce Merlin engines, this was one of the fastest piston-engined aircraft ever to go into production and it was the last of such aircraft to see front line service with the R.A.F. It had a long range and was intended for operations in the Pacific, but the war ended before it could take part. A two-seat, deck-landing version, the Sea Hornet, served with the Royal Navy until 1956. Maximum weight 12,880 lb; span 45 feet. *(right)*

## 1944: Bristol Brigand

Powered by two Bristol Centaurus engines of 2,500hp, the Brigand was designed primarily to take over the maritime strike duties being performed by the Beaufighter. With the collapse of Japan, however, the aircraft was eventually put into service as a light bomber designed to carry rockets as well as bombs. In this form the Brigand saw active service with the R.A.F. against terrorist activities in the Malayan jungle from 1950 to 1954. Maximum weight 39,000 lb; span 72 feet 4 inches. *(right)*

## 1945: Bristol Type 170

One of the most successful post-war British commercial aircraft was the Bristol Type 170 which appeared in two versions, the Freighter and the Wayfarer; both were powered by two Bristol Hercules engines. The Freighter, which had large clam-shell nose doors, could carry up to $5\frac{1}{2}$ tons, while the Wayfarer seated up to 34 passengers. A total of 214 Type 170s was built and they served world-wide with both civil and military operators. Maximum weight 44,000 lb; span 180 feet. *(above)*

## 1945: Hawker Sea Fury

This aeroplane, and its R.A.F. counterpart the Fury, were developments of the Tempest, the principal alteration being a reduction in the span by eliminating the centre section. The engine was a 2,480hp Bristol Centaurus. Production of the Fury was terminated at the end of the war, but the Sea Fury served with the Royal Navy until 1953. Sea Furies, operating from carriers, saw action in the Korean war. Maximum weight 12,500 lb; span 38 feet 5 inches. *(right centre)*

## 1945: Avro Tudor

Designed initially as an airliner for BOAC, but teething troubles and many modifications delayed production and eroded the performance. The aircraft, which was the first British airliner to be pressurised, eventually saw service with BSAA until the type was withdrawn following two accidents in the South Atlantic. Subsequently Tudors of various marks gave good service with charter companies, including some heavy duty with the Berlin airlift in 1948-49. Maximum weight (Tudor 4) 80,000 lb; span 120 feet. *"Flight" photo. (centre far right)*

## 1945: Vickers Viking

Britain's first post-war airliner, the Viking VC1, followed the tradition of the Vimy Commercial of 1919 in that the Viking design incorporated many major components of the Wellington and Warwick bombers. Fitted with two 1,690hp Bristol Hercules engines, the Viking carried 24 to 27 passengers and was extensively used by British

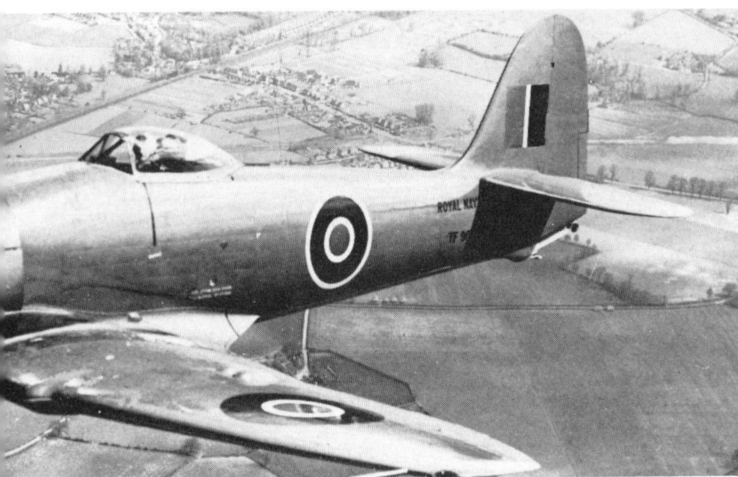

European Airways and by numerous overseas airlines. Four Vikings were supplied for the King's Flight. Maximum weight 34,000 lb; span 89 feet 3 inches. *(top)*

**1945: de Havilland Dove**
The first de Havilland civil aeroplane to emerge after the war was the DH104, appropriately named the Dove, a light transport aircraft with two 330hp Gipsy Queen engines and seats for up to eleven passengers. The Dove sold in large quantities all over the world, including the United States. Used at first mainly as a feeder liner and for charter work, the Dove also became popular as a business man's aircraft. It remained in production for 21 years. Maximum weight 9,150 lb; span 57 feet. *(right)*

# INTO THE JET AGE

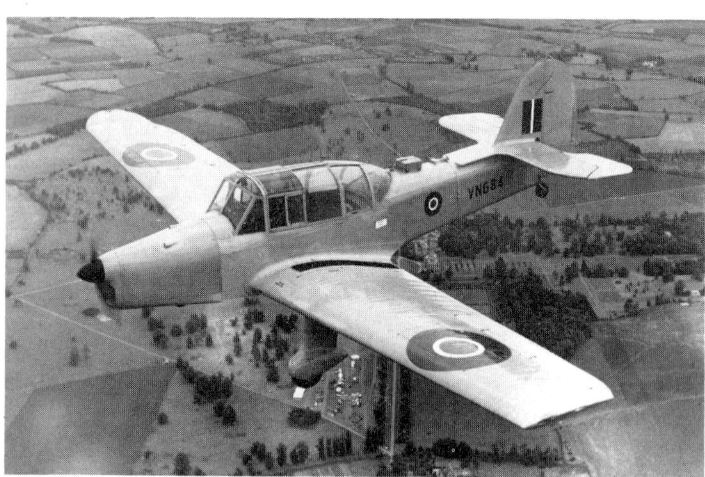

of Edinburgh and the Prince of Wales learned to fly in Chipmunks of the R.A.F. Maximum weight 2,000 lb; span 34 feet 4 inches. *(left-centre)*.

### 1946: Supermarine Attacker

The company's first jet aircraft was designed around the 5,000 lb thrust Rolls-Royce Nene engine. The Attacker, which was fitted with the wings of the Spiteful, was intended originally for the R.A.F. but was, in fact, adopted by the Royal Navy and by the Royal Pakistan Air Force. In 1948 the Attacker broke the world's record for the 100 km closed circuit at a speed of 564 mph. Maximum weight 11,500 lb; span 36 feet 11 inches. *"Flight" photo. (left)*.

### 1947: Armstrong Whitworth AW52

Two examples were built of this experimental aircraft designed to explore the possibilities of a large tailless airliner carrying passengers within the wing. It was powered by two Rolls-Royce Nene jet engines and had a laminar-flow wing with boundary-layer suction. After some 18 months' flying the first aircraft developed severe wing flutter and the pilot made the first-ever ejector-seat escape. Maximum weight 33,000 lb; span 90 feet. *(below)*

### 1947: Airspeed Ambassador

A most promising design, the Ambassador was badly delayed during production and thus

### 1946: Percival Prentice

Designed to Specification T23/43, the Prentice, with a 250 hp de Havilland Gipsy Queen engine, was the first Percival aircraft to have a fabric-covered, all-metal structure. It was adopted as the R.A.F.'s basic trainer and some 300 aircraft, designated the T.Mk 1, were delivered. The Prentice was also sold to Argentina, India and Lebanon. Rep'aced by the Provost by 1955, some Prentices were modified for civilian duties

with up to five seats. Maximum weight 4,200 lb; span 46 feet. *"Flight" photo. (above)*.

### 1946 de Havilland Chipmunk

An immigrant from de Havilland Canada, the DHC-1 was adopted by the R.A.F. as its standard elementary trainer and was put into large-scale production in Great Britain in 1949. In the R.A.F. it became the Chipmunk T.Mk 10 and was powered by a Gipsy Major engine of 145hp. Both the Duke

missed a potentially large market. Powered by two 2,625hp Bristol Centaurus engines, it had an outstanding single-engine performance. The pressurised cabin had seats for 47 passengers. The Ambassador went into operation with B.E.A. in 1952, known as the Elizabethan, and served with them until 1958. Some were later sold to other operators and remained in service into the 1970s. Maximum weight 52,000 lb; span 115 feet. *(left).*

**1949: de Havilland DH108**
Built to explore the possibilities of a tailless jet airliner. Three were built using the Vampire fuselage and the de Havilland Goblin engine. The first was a low-speed research aircraft, but the second was prepared for an attempt on the speed record, and it was in this that Geoffrey de Havilland junior lost his life in 1946. In 1948 the third DH108 was the first British aircraft to exceed the speed of sound. Maximum weight 8,960 lb; span 39 feet. *(above).*

### 1948: Hawker Sea Hawk

The first jet aircraft produced by Hawkers was a single-seat fighter powered by a Rolls-Royce Nene engine mounted centrally with bifurcated inlet and jet pipes. The initial batch of production Sea Hawks was built at Kingston, but the main production was undertaken by Armstrong Whitworth. The Sea Hawk served with the Royal Navy until 1960 and was also exported to Australia, Holland, India and West Germany. Maximum weight 13,220 lb; span 39 feet. *(right)*.

### 1948: Vickers Viscount

With four 1,990 ehp Rolls-Royce Dart engines, the Viscount was the world's first turbo-propeller airliner to operate passenger services and the first British airliner to make a significant penetration of the U.S. domestic

airline network. British European Airways and some 37 other airlines used Viscounts and total production amounted to 445 aircraft. The latest Viscount Type 810 carried up to 65 passengers and cruised at 357 mph. Maximum weight 72,500 lb; span 93 feet 8 inches. *(above)*.

### 1948: Percival Prince

Developed from the experimental Merganser, the Prince was intended for feeder-line and executive transport duties and a special model was designed for survey work. The Prince Series III was fitted with

two 550hp Alvis Leonides engines and carried eight passengers. In 1950 a version known as the Sea Prince entered service with the Royal Navy as a communications and training aircraft. Production eventually gave way to the larger Pembroke and President aircraft. Maximum weight 11,000 lb; span 56 feet. *"Flight" photo. (centre right)*

### 1948: Supermarine Seagull

The Type 318 Seagull was designed to specification S14/44 as an air-sea rescue amphibian to replace the Walrus and the Sea Otter. Only two prototypes were built, each being powered by a 1,815hp Rolls-Royce Griffon engine driving a six-blade, contra-rotating propeller. A feature of the Seagull was the variable-incidence wing with a range of movement of $10\frac{1}{2}$ deg, and with full-span slots and trailing-edge flaps. Maximum weight 14,500 lb; span 52 feet 6 inches. *"Flight" photo. (opposite page bottom).*

### 1949: English Electric Canberra

Britain's first jet bomber remained in production for more than ten years and was evolved through some 26 Marks, including those of tactical bomber, night intruder, photographic reconnaissance, trainer and unmanned target aircraft. The Canberra was built under licence in Australia and in the U.S.A. by the Martin company for the U.S.A.F. as the

B-57. Altogether, including overseas production, some 1,330 Canberras were built. Maximum weight (B Mk 6) 55,000 lb; length 65 feet 6 inches. *"Flight" photo. (bottom).*

### 1949: Armstrong Whitworth AW55 Apollo

A short to medium range airliner with four Armstrong Siddeley Mamba turbo-propeller engines and seats for 31 passengers. From the start the Apollo suffered from the undeveloped state of the Mamba engine; this, and other teething troubles which delayed tests, spoilt its chances of airline orders. Two Apollos were built and one was later used by the Empire Test Pilot's School at Farnborough. Maximum weight 47,000 lb; span 92 feet. *(top left).*

### 1949: Avro Shackleton

Designed as a long-range maritime reconnaissance aircraft, it entered service in 1951 and formed the main equipment of Coastal Command, R.A.F., until largely superseded by the Nimrod. The Shackleton was also used by the South African Air Force. Progressively modified, the Shackleton MR3, with four Rolls-Royce Griffon engines, had a range of more than 4,200 miles and could remain airborne for up to 24 hours. Maximum weight 100,000 lb; span 120 feet. *(left).*

### 1949: Vickers Valetta and Varsity

From the civil Vickers Viking were developed two military aircraft, the Valetta, a troop carrier to replace the Dakota, and the Varsity as an aircrew trainer. This latter differed in having an increased span, a nose wheel undercarriage and a bomb-aimer's prone position in a ventral pannier. Both types had two Bristol Hercules engines. A total of 426 Valettas and Varsities was built. Maximum weight (Varsity, right) 37,500 lb; span 95 feet 7 inches.

### 1949: de Havilland DH112 Venom

Designed as an interim fighter to fill the gap between the first jet fighters and the new generation being developed. Based on the Vampire layout, the Venom had the more powerful de Havilland Ghost engine and a thinner wing. It was built as a single-seat fighter-bomber and as a two-seat night fighter for the R.A.F. and as the Sea Venom all-weather fighter for the Navy. Maximum weight 15,400 lb; span 41 feet 8 inches. *(right)*

### 1949: Bristol Type 167 Brabazon

Designed to carry 100 passengers on transatlantic routes, and built before today's high take-off and landing speeds became acceptable, the Brabazon had a range of more than 5,500 miles at a cruising speed of 250 mph and could take off from runways of less than 2,000 yards. Power was supplied by eight 2,500hp Bristol Centaurus engines in coupled pairs driving contra-rotating propellers. The Brabazon was broken up in 1953. Maximum weight 290,000 lb; span 230 feet. *"Flight" photo. (opposite page top)*

### 1949: de Havilland Comet

After the war de Havilland, almost alone among aircraft manufacturers, appreciated the commercial possibilities of the jet engine, and the DH106 Comet was the world's first airliner to be so powered. At one step it virtually doubled the speed of air travel and set new standards of comfort. After the accidents of 1954 the structure was modified and in 1958 the Comet 4 opened the first regular jet service to the U.S.A. Maximum weight (Comet 4) 162,000 lb; span 114 feet 10 inches. *(right centre)*

### 1950: de Havilland DH114 Heron

Offered as "an airliner in miniature", the Heron was an enlarged version of the Dove with four 250hp Gipsy Queen engines and seats for 17 passengers. In the interest of cheapness and simplicity the first Herons had a fixed undercarriage but this proved unpopular and subsequent marks had retractable gear. The Heron sold world-wide as an airliner and as a business aircraft and three served with the Queen's Flight. Maximum weight 13,500 lb; span 71 feet 6 inches. *(below)*

### 1950: Percival Provost

The Hunting Percival Provost two-seat trainer was designed to meet a Ministry of Supply Specification 16/48 and was selected to replace the Percival Prentice as the basic trainer for the R.A.F. The prototype had an Armstrong Siddeley Cheetah engine but production aircraft were powered by a 550hp Alvis Leonides radial engine. An armed version, the T Mk 53, was supplied to a number of overseas air forces. Maximum weight 4,400 lb; span 35 feet 2 inches. *"Flight" photo. (bottom right)*

## 1950: Scottish Aviation Pioneer

The Pioneer first flew in 1947 as a civil aircraft with a de Havilland Gipsy Queen engine but was redesigned, appearing in 1950 as a five-seater with a 540hp Alvis Leonides for the R.A.F. The Pioneer II, with full-span flaps and leading-edge slots had an exceptional STOL performance and a stalling speed of 36 mph. Pioneers were used by the R.A.F., particularly in Malaya, and others served with the Ceylon Air Force. Maximum weight 5,800 lb; span 49 feet 9 inches. *(bottom)*.

## 1950: Blackburn Beverley

This aircraft started life as the General Aircraft Universal Freighter, and joined the R.A.F. in 1956. With its four Bristol Centaurus engines, the Beverley could uplift nearly 25 tons of

## 1951: Hawker Hunter

The Hunter has proved to be one of the most versatile jet fighters to see service with the R.A.F. With a total production of nearly 2,000 aircraft, it sold extensively abroad and is still in use by many overseas air forces. Current Hunters are powered by Rolls-Royce Avons, but some built by Armstrong Whitworth, had Sapphire engines. When superseded as fighters the R.A.F.'s Hunters were re-deployed as trainers. Maximum weight 18,090 lb; span 33 feet 8 inches. *(right)*.

## 1951: Vickers Valiant

The first of the R.A.F.'s V-bombers to be produced; it was ordered in November 1949 and was first flown in May 1951. With four 10,000 lb thrust Rolls-

freight in its capacious hold; in addition there were seats for 36 passengers in the tail boom. Beverleys saw service with the R.A.F. at home and in the Middle East, Africa and the Far East before they were finally withdrawn in 1968. Maximum weight 135,000 lb; span 162 feet. *(top left)*.

Royce Avon engines, the Valiant had a speed of 567 mph at 30,000 feet. It went into action in the 1956 Suez campaign and it was a Valiant which, in 1957, dropped Britain's first H-bomb. A total of 107 Valiants were built. Maximum weight 140,000 lb; span 114 feet 4 inches. *(bottom right)*.

## 1952: Supermarine Swift

The Swift was originally intended as a fighter but, after a long period of development, its role with the R.A.F. was changed to that of fast tactical reconnaissance duties. In this form the Swift Mk V first flew in May 1955 and entered service with the R.A.F. about a

year later. In September 1953 a Swift Mk IV broke the World's Speed Record by achieving an average speed over a 3-km course of 735·7 mph. Maximum weight 21,400 lb; Length 41 feet 6 inches. *(above far right)*.

## 1951: Gloster Javelin

The Javelin was the first delta-wing aircraft to enter service with the R.A.F., which it did in February 1956 after a number of modifications had been introduced. Designed as an all-weather fighter, the Javelin was developed through numerous Marks, the Mk 9 having two Armstrong Siddeley Sapphire engines of 11,000 lb thrust. Armament consisted of Aden guns and de Havilland Firestreak missiles. Maximum weight 43,165 lb; span 52 feet. *(top left).*

## 1952: Bristol Britannia

The last of the large propeller airliners, the Britannia first flew in August 1952. Powered by four 3,780hp Bristol Proteus turbo-propeller engines, the Britannia carried up to 139 passengers and had a range of 4,270 miles. Operated by B.O.A.C., R.A.F. Transport Command and some other national airlines, the Britannia proved itself to be one of the most reliable airliners, some of which achieved an annual utilisation of more than 4,000 hours. Maximum weight 185,000 lb; span 142 feet 3 inches. *(top right).*

## 1952: Avro Vulcan

The world's first large delta-wing bomber, designed to carry a nuclear weapon, and the Avro Blue Steel stand-off bomb, at near-sonic speeds. Ordered in quantity for Bomber Command R.A.F., the Vulcan entered service in 1956 and has many air-refuelled long-distance flights to its credit, including that by three aircraft from England to Perth in Western Australia in 1963. The B Mk.2 Vulcan is powered by four Rolls-Royce Bristol Olympus engines. Maximum weight 204,000 lb; span 99 feet. *(right).*

## 1954: Percival Jet Provost

A direct descendant of the Provost, the Hunting Percival Jet Provost, powered by a Bristol Siddeley Viper engine giving 1,750 lb of thrust, used the wings and tailplane of the Provost, suitably modified, but had a retractable nosewheel undercarriage. The Jet Provost Mk III, ordered in quantity, entered service in 1959 as the R.A.F.'s first jet *ab initio* trainer. The Jet Provost was adopted by several overseas air forces, including those of Ceylon, Sudan and Kuwait. Maximum weight 6,195 lb; span 36 feet 11 inches. *"Flight" photo. (right).*

## 1957: de Havilland Sea Vixen

Developed from the DH110 which first flew in 1951 and which was in competition with the Gloster Javelin for the R.A.F.'s all-weather fighter contract. Re-designed with folding wings, a strengthened undercarriage, a deck-landing hook and other modifications, the first production Sea Vixen, with two Rolls-Royce Avon engines, flew in 1957 and subsequently entered service with the Royal Navy for all-weather fighting and strike reconnaissance duties. Maximum weight 35,000 lb; length 53 feet 7 inches. *(far right).*

### 1953: English Electric Lightning

The R.A.F.'s first truly supersonic fighter, the prototype having flown faster than sound on its third flight, in August 1954. Powered by two Rolls-Royce Avon engines and with a wing sweep of 60 deg, the Lightning has a top speed exceeding 1,500 mph and can reach Mach 0·9 at 40,000 feet in 3½ minutes. The Lightning entered service with the R.A.F. in 1959 and is still in frontline service over 20 years later. Maximum weight 41,700 lb; length 55 feet 3 inches. *"Flight" photo. (above).*

### 1955: Scottish Aviation Twin Pioneer

This general transport aircraft carried up to 18 passengers or 4,000 lb of freight. The Series 3, with two 640hp Alvis Leonides engines and full-span flaps and leading edge slots, had an outstanding STOL performance with a take-off and a landing run of only some 550 feet. The Twin Pioneer found a ready market with operators in many parts of the world and 40 were supplied to the R.A.F. Maximum weight 14,600 lb; span 76 feet 6 inches. *(above right).*

### 1956: Supermarine Scimitar

Built as a replacement for the Sea Hawk, the Supermarine Scimitar was the first of the Royal Navy's carrier-borne, single-seat strike fighters to have swept wings, power controls and blown flaps. Armament consisted of four 30-mm guns and rockets carried below the wings; in the strike role the Scimitar could carry a tactical nuclear bomb. The Scimitar, powered by a 11,250-lb thrust Rolls-Royce Avon engine, was supersonic in a dive. Length 56 feet 2 inches. *(top right).*

### 1958: Blackburn Buccaneer

Designed as high-speed, low-level strike aircraft, the first Buccaneers were powered by two de Havilland Gyron Junior engines, but the Mk 2 has Rolls-Royce Speys. Notable features of the Buccaneer are the thin-section high-speed wing with boundary-layer control and the "area-rule" design of the fuselage. The Buccaneer served with the Royal Navy and the South African Air Force and with the R.A.F. Maximum weight 56,000 lb; length 63 feet 5 inches. *(right).*

### 1959: Armstrong Whitworth Argosy

The Argosy was a freight-carrying aircraft with front and rear doors to its large-capacity hold. Powered by four Rolls-Royce Dart turbo-propeller engines, it carried more than 30,000 lb of cargo. First orders came from Riddle Airlines of America and British European Airways also employed Argosies, some of which were the improved Series 220 model. Another version, specially adapted for military use, served with the R.A.F. Maximum weight (Series 220) 93,000 lb; span 115 feet. *(centre right).*

## 1959: Vickers Vanguard

The Vanguard, a larger version of the Viscount designed to carry up to 139 passengers, was powered by four Rolls-Royce Tyne turbo-propeller engines. The Vanguard went into service with British European Airways in March 1961 and later with Trans-Canada Air Lines. Although proving highly economical, the Vanguard inevitably had to give way to the pure jet airliner and eventually most of the 44 Vanguards built were converted to freighters. Maximum weight 141,000 lb; span 118 feet. *(above)*.

## 1959: Folland Gnat

This advanced trainer, made famous throughout Europe by reason of the demonstrations given by the Red Arrows formation aerobatic team of the R.A.F., is powered by a Rolls-Royce Bristol Orpheus engine giving 4,230 lb of thrust. The trainer, which is capable of trans-sonic speeds, is a two-seat version of the original Gnat light fighter which was first flown in 1955 and which was exported to India and Finland. Maximum weight 8,985 lb; span 24 feet. *(top)*.

## 1960: HS 748

Of the many attempts to produce a "Dakota replacement", one of the most successful is the HS 748, the 48-passenger airliner now in service world-wide with more than 60 operators. In its latest form, the HS 748-2B, with Rolls-Royce Dart 536-2 engines which give more power for hot or high airfields, offers up to 2,000 lb more payload from limiting airfields together with a reduction of some 9 per cent in block fuel consumption. Maximum weight 45,000 lb; span 102 feet 6 inches. *(top right)*.

## 1962: Vickers VC10

This airliner, with four rear-mounted Rolls-Royce Conway engines and a clean, uncluttered wing, had an outstanding airfield performance and a cruising speed of 580 mph. It

proved exceedingly popular with passengers. Two versions were built, the VC10 which carried 135 passengers, and the Super VC10 which seated 28 more and which was used on the Atlantic services. VC10s were bought by B.O.A.C., R.A.F. Transport Command and several overseas operators. Maximum weight 335,000 lb; span 146 feet 2 inches. *British Airways photo. (opposite page centre).*

### 1962: HS 125

Built to provide the business man with the advantages of a private aircraft combined with the speed of a jet airliner, the HS 125 has undergone continuous development culminating in the series 700. Powered by two quiet Garrett-Airesearch engines, the Series 700 has a range of 2,650 statute miles and seats 8-10 passengers in a comfortable lounge-style cabin. By 1980 sales neared 500 aircraft with some 250 going to America. Maximum weight 24,200 lb; span 47 feet. *(left).*

## 1962: Trident

The Trident has been produced in three main versions for B.E.A. and other airlines. All are powered by three Rolls-Royce Spey engines, the Trident 3, the largest, capable of carrying up to 170 passengers, having in addition a Rolls-Royce lightweight boost engine for short take-off. The Trident was the first airliner in the world to introduce automatic landing in regular airline service. Maximum weight (Trident 3) 155,000 lb; span 98 feet. *(right).*

## 1963: BAC. One-Eleven

Britain's best-selling twin-jet airliner; now operating world-wide, including the U.S.A. it is available in several variants. The Series 500, illustrated, has accommodation for 119 passengers. Another development, the 475, is a high-performance aircraft suitable for short airfields. All variants have two Rolls-Royce Spey engines. Rumania is manufacturing One-Elevens under licence. Maximum weight (Series 500) 91,000 lb; span 93 feet 6 inches. *(far right).*

## 1966: Harrier

The Harrier V/STOL jet fighter, which introduces an entirely new concept into military aviation, is now in service with the R.A.F., the U.S. Marine Corps and the Spanish Navy. A modified version, the Sea Harrier, joined the Royal Navy in 1979. With its Rolls-Royce Pegasus engine developing 21,500 lb of thrust, the Harrier can operate from a space little larger than itself and fly at trans-sonic speeds. Maximum weight 26,000 lb; length 45 feet 6 inches. *(above).*

### 1967: Nimrod

The world's first jet-propelled maritime reconnaissance aircraft, the Nimrod entered service with the R.A.F. in 1969 as a replacement for the Avro Shackleton. Based on the well-tried airframe of the Comet jet airliner, the Nimrod, with its four Rolls-Royce Spey by-pass jet engines, combines a high transit speed with the ability to patrol economically at sea level with two of its engines shut down. Maximum weight (MRI) 177,500 lb; span 114 feet 9 inches. *(right)*.

### 1967: Strikemaster

The Strikemaster, a development of the Jet Provost, is a basic and advanced trainer with a crew of two seated side-by-side in a pressurised cockpit; it can also be used in the tactical support role. With an up-rated Rolls-Royce Viper engine giving 3,410 lb of thrust, the Strikemaster can carry 3,000 lb of bombs or rockets and two machine guns. The Strikemaster has been supplied to numerous national air forces. Maximum weight 11,500 lb; span 36 feet 10 inches. *(right)*.

### 1967: Jetstream

The Jetstream light turbo-propeller, transport aircraft originally produced by the Handley Page company, was taken over by Scottish Aviation in 1972 and deliveries to civil customers and the R.A.F. continued until 1976. In 1978 British Aerospace announced a new version, the Jetstream 31, due to fly in 1979 and powered by two 940 shp Garrett AiResearch engines and carrying up to 18 passengers. The Jetstream 31 will be suitable for commuter, corporate or military duties. Maximum weight 14,000 lb; span 52 feet. *(above far right)*.

### 1969: Jaguar

This low-level, strike and reconnaissance aircraft, built jointly by British Aerospace and Dassault-Breguet is in service with the British, French and Indian air forces. The Jaguar is supersonic at all altitudes, has a range of 1,800 miles and a maximum weapon load of 10,000 lb. Power is supplied by two Rolls-Royce Turbomeca Adour engines, each giving 7,380 lb of thrust with reheat. Maximum weight 34,000 lb; length 55 feet 3 inches. *(below)*.

## 1971: Bulldog

The Bulldog 120 basic trainer is in service with the R.A.F. and a number of other overseas air forces. Powered by a 200hp Avco-Lycoming engine, the Bulldog is normally a side-by-side two-seater but a third seat can be fitted. The aircraft is fully aerobatic and, with a variety of underwing stores, it can also be used for weapon training, light strike, supply dropping and other duties. Maximum weight 2,238 lb; span 33 feet. *(above)*.

## 1972: Airbus A300

A wide-bodied airliner built jointly by six European nations with British Aerospace responsible for the wing. This is of advanced aerodynamic design and, with the two economical fan engines, is largely responsible for the aircraft's superior economic performance. The A300 B2 and B4 are in service with the smaller A310 due in 1982. Together they represent a family of airliners with ranges and payloads covering a wide spectrum of operational requirements. Maximum weight (B2) 313,000 lb; span 147 feet. *(above centre)*.

### 1969: Concorde

The Anglo-French Concorde, the world's first airliner to begin supersonic passenger services, started operation with British Airways and Air France in January 1976. Built jointly by British Aerospace and Aerospatiale, the Concorde is powered by four 39,000 lb thrust Rolls-Royce/SNECMA Olympus engines, cruises at Mach 2, about 1,350 mph, and has a range exceeding 4,000 miles. Journey time between London and New York is about $3\frac{1}{2}$ hours. Maximum weight 408,000 lb; length 203 feet 9 inches. *(right).*

### 1974: Hawk

The Hawk basic and advanced trainer was designed to replace the Gnat and Hunter trainers of the R.A.F. With one 5,440 lb thrust Rolls-Royce Turbomeca Adour engine, the Hawk can exceed Mach 1 in a dive and is suitable for radio, navigation and weapon training and can be equipped for ground attack and other operational roles. The Hawk is in service with the R.A.F. and is being supplied to several other air forces. Maximum weight 17,097 lb; length 38 feet 11 inches. *(above).*

### 1974: Tornado

This multi-role combat aircraft is an all-weather, swing-wing machine being built by the tri-national company Panavia, in Great Britain, Germany and Italy. Designed to fulfil a multiplicity of roles, including close support, interdiction and air superiority, the Tornado, with two 15,000 lb thrust Turbo-Union RB199 engines, has a speed of more than 1,320 mph. The F2 air-defence variant is being developed for the R.A.F. Maximum weight 58,000 lb; length 54 feet 10 inches. *(top right).*

ZA254
ZA254
TORNADO
F-2

British airways

# Master of the Art

By **J M RAMSDEN** CEng FRAeS FSLAET FRSA Editor *Flight International*

No single nation, no one company, can claim to write the autobiography of the aeroplane. Aviation is an international industry, more so today than ever; and the high human accomplishment of flight has been the work of all mankind. But in this chronicle we appreciate one company's uniquely complete mastery of the art.

British Aerospace—BAe for short—has spread wings which span virtually the whole technical history of airframe pioneering and commerce.

The cutting edge—which perfectionist man must always make sharper than he needs—is Concorde. For the British and French aircraft industries and airlines, and for their competitors, this supersonic transport provides the ultimate measure of passenger speed in safety and comfort.

These aviation commodities were first marketed internationally (London-Paris) by a D.H.4A, the product of a BAe forebear, in 1919.

What the superpowers have as yet only attempted Europe has achieved: Concorde has been in daily international scheduled service since January 1976. It halves travel for those whose time is money. Airworthy supersonic public transport was as challenging to Europe's spirit and intellect as was Apollo to America.

Commerce and industry cannot thrive on prowess alone. A £3,000 million BAe sales ledger (military and civil) measures the extent to which pride, skill and risk are being annually cashed as profit.

Europe's two biggest industrial undertakings are Tornado and Airbus, and both have been founded with British Aerospace as a leading partner.

Tornado, with the Germans and Italians, is a strike-fighter without equivalent in the superpower weapon inventories. Eight hundred or more are on order. Tornado's name may one day be joined with the fame of such combat classics—all from BAe's family tree—as the Sopwith Camel, SE.5a,

Vickers-Supermarine Spitfire, de Havilland Vampire, Gloster Meteor, Hawker Hurricane, de Havilland Mosquito, Hawker Hunter, and English Electric Lightning and Canberra. Something of all these illustrious military types is in the genes of Tornado.

More than a combat aircraft, Tornado is also the reconciliation of European skills which in the past have been perverted into fighting or bombing Europeans.

Airbus too is a European collegiate, the joint work of the British, Dutch, French, German and Spanish aircraft industries. Like Tornado, Airbus was launched into a market gap; nobody else had coupled twin-engined safety and fuel-efficiency to twin-aisle passenger appeal. It is now one of few airliners seriously to challenge American suppliers, with around 400 sold to more than 40 customers.

"Give me the wing, and I will give you the aeroplane," is the undeniable aphorism which gives British Aerospace its place in Airbus. The company's main contribution to the A300, and to its A310 sistership, is wing design and production.

The whole Airbus has been endowed by a European airliner culture which has been both innovating and commercial.

British Aerospace or its predecessors were the first with a passenger jet, the de Havilland Comet 1, in 1952; the first with a passenger turboprop, the Vickers Viscount, in 1953 (more than 400 sold); the first with a transatlantic jet airliner, the Comet 4, in 1958; the first with a trijet, the Trident, in 1964; and the first with a twinjet, the One-Eleven, in 1965 (more than 200 sold).

The twin-turboprop BAe 748 is in its third decade of demand (more than 350 sold) and its turbofan BAe 146 successor is now winning orders for 1983 service.

Light transport and training aircraft, civil and military, have always been a British proficiency, and are strongly so today. In the Scottish Bulldog we find the good tempers and guts of such classic primary trainers—all the work of BAe ancestors—as the 1946

Chipmunk, the 1932 Tiger Moth and the 1914 Avro 504K. The company's most accomplished expression of the postgraduate art is the Hawk, the handling precision of which is consummately displayed by the RAF Red Arrows aerobatic team.

The BAe 125 company jet is the fastest seller in the civil shop (some 500 to date). This light transport, and its newer turboprop sister the Jetstream, inherit the tough elegance of many hundred Dragon Rapides, Doves and Herons which, from the 'thirties to the 'sixties, initiated small operators into the economy and efficiency of air transport.

In Nimrod, especially in the new AEW command-post, BAe attains the highest systems technology and the industrial discipline required to obtain, process, communicate, protect and present information.

Such discipline is particularly exacting in spaceflight, a field in which BAe Dynamics excels—not least in commercial satellites for maritime and intercontinental communications.

Another witness to the maritime instincts and needs of the British are the anti-missile Seawolf and anti-ship Sea Skua missiles. These BAe Dynamics products, and Sea Harrier, represent the most seachanging innovations since the broadside of Henry VIII's day.

Shipborne Sea Harrier is the newest version of the world's only proven fixed-wing vertical take-off aircraft. BAe's land-based Harrier has been in RAF service since 1969 and—the only imported combat aircraft in American operation since the Canberra— with the US Marines. In Harrier and Sea Harrier, British Aerospace and Rolls-Royce have realised the commander's dream of high-performance combat aircraft independent of vulnerable runways and giant aircraft carriers.

With the ground-to-air Rapier and air-to-air Sky Flash missiles, the still unique Harrier family completes one company's unequalled mastery of the aviation art.

---

*A Royal Navy Sea Harrier FRS.1 prepares to alight on the 50ft by 81ft helicopter platform of the Royal Fleet Auxiliary* Olwen. *The revolutionary Harrier remains the only operational vertical take-off aircraft in the world, and sales prospects for the multi-role Sea Harrier look promising*

**Opposite page**

*To celebrate HS 125 business jet sales reaching 400—more than 200 of them to North American customers—14 aircraft gather at British Aerospace Chester, led by the 700 Series with fuel-efficient Garrett AiResearch turbofans, which give this latest version greater range for less noise*

50
ROYAL NAVY

BRS AIR LONDON
G-BSAA
G-BBEP
G-5-13
G-AVOI
G-BFAN
125 700